Diversity, Equity, Inclusion, and Belonging Field Guide: Stories of Lived Experience

I0095604

Edited by

Rita Yerkes, EdD

Denise Mitten, PhD

Karen Warren, PhD

association for
experiential education
www.aee.org

Diversity, Equity, Inclusion, and Belonging Field Guide: Stories of Lived Experience project team members

Project director

Sky Gray

Project core members

Sherry Bagley, Bobbi Beale, Sky Gray, Denise Mitten, Christine Norton, Karen Warren, and Rita Yerkes

Project members

Susie Barr-Wilson, Dani Beale, Monique Brand, George McDonald, Hossein Ordabodian, Tanya Rao, Alyssa Roberts, The Roberts family, Bob Stanton, Sändra J. Washington, and Sharon J. Washington

First paperback edition October 2022
Book cover design by Monique Brand, Red-tailed Hawk by Dudley Edmondson
ISBN 979-8-9871020-0-8 (paperback)
ISBN 979-8-9871020-1-5 (ebook)

www.aee.org

Table of Contents

Acknowledgements ii

Family Dedication iv

    My Sister, Nina vi

Foreward ix

    Foreward x

Introduction 1

    Introduction 2

Reflection Papers 9

    A Mirror and A Door 10

    The Association for Experiential Education's Evolving Journey
        Toward Diversity, Equity, Inclusion, and Belonging 14

    The Picnic Table at the 1983 AEE Conference 18

    The Road to Justice is Long 23

    Viewed as An Alien: Race-based Assumptions in the
        Outdoors 28

    Diversity Awareness as a Mindset: Doing What We Can
        Where We Can 32

    From Urban Spaces to Wild Places: 45 years of Connecting
        Youth of Color to Natural Landscapes 38

    The Woods 44

    Without Gender 46

    Building a Foundation of Trust 51

    Color the Parks Fantastic! 55

    Mainstreams and Margins 57

    Reflections on My Experience Developing the First Indigenous
        Youth Program to be Recognized as Evidenced-based 60

    Reflections on the Glass Ceiling: Then and Now 64

    Resiliency Rising 71

    Be the Change: Speaking Up, Stepping in It (Sometimes),
        and Being an Ally 74

    The Other Side of the Mountain 78

    Rock Climbing and Diversity, Equity, Inclusion, and
        Belonging Lessons 81

    Bold Not Bossy: Asking Girls to Lead in Outdoor Spaces (and
        Beyond) 86

Reflections on Diversity and Inclusion in AEE 92

The Never-Ending Quest for Safety and Belonging 96

Is the Outdoors Gendered? 102

Overcoming "Not Enough": A Pathway to Inclusivity 111

We Still Have Work to Do 115

Is Distinguished What We Really Seek? 120

When Actions Speak Louder Than a Mission Statement:
    Personal Reflection on Diversity, Inclusion, Equity and a
    Sense of Belonging 126

Reflections on Social Justice 132

Experiential Education and the Aha Moment 136

Understanding Justice, Equity, Diversity and Inclusion as a
    Young Person of Color 140

Honoring Women's Voices 144

Justice and Joy 148

A Testimonio of Transformational Justice 150

Understanding the Perceptions African Americans Have
    About the Environment and Nature and How These
    Perceptions Influence Their Behavior and
    Environmental Commitment 157

Towards Global Inclusion and Belonging 163

Travel with Purpose: International Service-Learning in Costa
    Rica 168

Stay Humble and Stay Curious 174

Nina Roberts: A Remembrance...184

Call to Action 188

    Call to Action 189

Definition of Terms 192

    Definition of Terms 193

Social Justice Quotes 214

    Social Justice Quotes 215

Contributor Biographies 223

The Association for Experiential Education

We believe learning through experience positively transforms people and our world. The Association for Experiential Education (AEE) is a nonprofit professional membership association dedicated to experiential education and the students, educators, and practitioners who utilize its philosophy. We provide a global community with networking, education, research, and standards for people who use experiential education in their work. Who are these people? Classroom teachers, camp counselors, adventure therapists, college professors, corporate trainers, expedition leaders, social and emotional learning providers, social justice advocates, and more.

As an organization we hold these values:

Global Community
Adventure and Challenge
Reflective Leadership
Social Justice
The Natural World
Creative Play

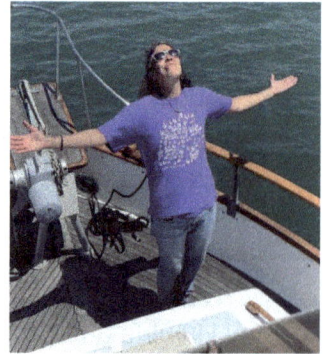

Photo courtesy of Sky Gray

Dr. Nina Roberts was a long-time member and an active volunteer leader in AEE for several decades. Her vision for what an inclusive organization could look like helped push us forward. Her support and determination led to significant advancements for all of us.

AEE is proud to offer this DEIB Field Guide in honor of Nina. Proceeds from the sale of this book will go into a fund created in her honor—The Dr. Nina Roberts Social Justice fund. This fund will provide members with resources to further their DEIB journeys. Visit www.aee.org to find out more.

Acknowledgements

Putting together the Diversity, Equity, Inclusion, and Belonging Field Guide: Stories of Lived Experience has been a labor of love and a cathartic journey. This field guide is born from hard work, grief, joy, and the desire to carry Nina's torch. We would like to thank and acknowledge the many volunteers who have been involved in this process.

Foremost, thank you to the authors of the reflection papers. These individuals had the courage to share their lived experiences. Their commitment to social justice shows up in their heart-felt stories. They represent some of the many people dedicated to advancing diversity, equity, inclusion, and belonging in the outdoor and experiential education fields.

Since April 2022, the core committee of devoted carriers of the torch met regularly to share emotional and project updates. Sky Gray, as the project director, was the connective tissue and the keeper of the spirit and intent of Nina's idea. Project core members include Sherry Bagley, Bobbi Beale, Denise Mitten, Christine Norton, Karen Warren, and Rita Yerkes. It is quite incredible that 6 months later we have the Diversity, Equity, Inclusion, and Belonging Field Guide.

Thank you, Sherry Bagley, Executive Director of the Association for Experiential Education. Sherry provided many resources and the means to make this project come to fruition. Her support and drive for this field guide were unwavering.

The meticulous and devoted editors, Rita Yerkes, Karen Warren, and Denise Mitten worked countless hours with the writers to help hone their stories into the beautiful pieces that they have become.

Hossein Ordabodian graciously provided copy editing.

Thanks to Pam Firth from The Detail Devil for formatting consultation.

Christine Norton created and initiated the call for quotes and reflection papers, collaborated on the introduction and provided support throughout the project.

Monique Brand was the graphic artist extraordinaire for the field guide and was inspired to be part of this project because of her cousin, Nina.

Dudley Edmondson provided the red-tailed hawk photo for the cover.

Dani and Bobbie Beale collected, organized, and authenticated the social justice quotes.

Susie Barr-Wilson and Tanya Rao organized and compiled definitions for the glossary of terms. The Arvana Group, Foundation for a Healthy St. Pete, Ongig, The Safe Zone Project, and World Trust provided support.

George McDonald, the Chief of Youth Programs and the Experienced Services Program Division with the National Park Service supported connections with many of our authors.

Bob Stanton, Sändra J. Washington, and Sharon J. Washington thoughtfully wrote the opening and closing papers for this field guide.

And thank you so much to Alyssa Roberts and the entire Roberts family for their encouragement and support.

Family Dedication

Photo courtesy of Alyssa Roberts

My Sister, Nina

Alyssa Roberts

My sister Nina will forever be identified by her words and deeds for equity relating to parks and public lands. Her passion for environmental justice and love of the outdoors was incredible. I know she was well published and nationally recognized in her field. Yes, she was a Fulbright Scholar. And I recognize she wasan amazing and sought-after speaker. But to me she was a cool sister and even a better friend. Nina pushed boundaries and buttons—she could be argumentative and stubborn. And although she did not have children, she never hesitated in advising me with my own two. Still, her laughter was contagious and her love of life extraordinary. Nina also pushed, in a good way, for play and spontaneity. When she was on sabbatical in 2016 in Washington, D.C. near where I live, she would call me in the middle of the day and invite me to a concert or show that evening. I would pause—last minute? On a "school" night? Oh, this was out of my routine. But Nina wouldn't take no for an answer and I'm glad. When I was with Nina life was never dull. I credit her for my collection of ticket stubs, wonderful photos, and many fond memories.

Nina's primary focus in her career was on experiential learning and connecting urban communities with public lands. While expanding the use of outdoor spaces for diverse populations was her expertise and passion, it was also personal. As part of a mixed-race family, Nina learned early on that overt and covert racism perpetuated a lack of diversity in many areas of life. As someone who enjoyed the outdoors and advocated for public land use, she was committed to breaking down barriers of inequality in outdoor recreation opportunities. Nina knew that parks are important to our country's well-being and that public spaces had to be accessible and inclusive for everyone. She advocated for recreation and an appreciation for our natural resources. Long before there were "prescriptions for nature walks," Nina recognized that access to parks and open spaceswas good for a person's health and community. And not just access, but diversity in planning committees and leadership aswell.

Nina never missed an opportunity to learn about and explore a park. She was as knowledgeable about the outdoors as she was comfortable in the outdoors. No matter the venue—a pocket park, city park, or national park—her knowledge and enthusiasmwere unparalleled.

Some of my favorite memories of time with Nina were formed as we drove cross country from San Francisco to Washington, D.C. Never shy with her opinions, we had lots of interesting conversations about race, ethnicity, and culture. As sisters and friends do, we also shared our favorite music, gossiped about family, and talked about our futures together.

Our lists of things to do and see on our trip revolved around, of course, parks and enjoying outdoor spaces. Nina had traversed the country several times, but it was my first cross country roadtrip and an opportunity to see and enjoy our country's breathtaking and varied landscapes. Being with Nina was like having a personal tour guide. It was my first-time seeing Mt. Rushmore, Crazy Horse, Devil's Tower, and the Badlands. We strolled the Truckee River Walk in Reno and hiked in Targhee National Forest in Montana. We relished time together in Sioux Falls State Park, the Dells in Wisconsin, and Cuyahoga National Park in Cleveland. We visited friends and family along the way. Itwas, in sum, incredible. I will be forever grateful and honored that Nina asked me to take this trip with her. Nina faced her diagnosis just as she did other parts of her life— with a positive attitude. She never complained although she had every right to. Even as her disease progressed, she pushed on to make one more cross-country road trip. With waning energy, she would still sit in her garden, her private oasis, and work on her laptop to complete projects and converse with students. In her final days, Nina's wish was to spend time outdoors. Our brother helped her out of her house one afternoon and she sat in the fresh air surrounded by her siblings. My last photo of Nina is of her outside, sunshine and a smile on her face.

Photo courtesy of the Roberts Family

Foreword

Photo courtesy of Robbie Francis

Foreword

Bob Stanton

My introduction to the National Park Service (NPS) was as a seasonal ranger at Grand Teton in 1962. There were very few Black park rangers working for NPS at that time and my opportunity was part of a concerted effort by then-Secretary of Interior Stewart Udall to diversify the workforce of the NPS. This initial experience eventually led to my 35-year NPS career. Early in my career, the welcome I received from senior staff at Grand Teton during the height of the Civil Rights Movement made a lasting impression. It is because of dedicated staff, volunteers, and those who love the parks that change is made. Throughout my association with national parks, I've felt strongly that the workforce and programs of NPS should represent the face of America. I know that Dr. Nina Roberts and I shared this core belief. During my tenure with NPS, I took particular interest in increasing the diversity of Park Service staff and public programs to promote opportunities for young people to engage with our parks. I've worked with hundreds of good people over the course of my career, and I was blessed to hire and work with Dr. Roberts who had energy, passion, and drive unmatched in many ways.

When it comes to real action with regards to diversity, equity, inclusion and belonging (DEIB), sometimes people get tired and discouraged, and can lose hope waiting for change. That was not the case with my longtime friend and colleague Dr. Roberts, who remained deeply passionate and even joyful in her work to make sure outdoor spaces were welcoming of our nation's rich diversity. Dr. Roberts' life's work and legacy is one to be hailed, promoted, and never forgotten. The heart of this field guide represents very well her keen interest in people telling their truths and sharing their stories. She dreamed this field guide would reach multiple audiences and her dream has come true. Let us embrace as our individual and collective responsibility a commitment to build upon Dr. Roberts' contributions, vision, and enduring legacy. The field guide provides excellent counsel in our going forward.

Lastly, I want to acknowledge Dr. Roberts' passion and hard work toward increasing the involvement of our youth in the preservation of the nation's rich and diverse natural and cultural resources. Truly, she was filled with the spirit of Dr. Mary McLeod Bethune who would remind us:

> The world around us really belongs to our youth, for youth will take over its future management. Our youth must never lose their zeal for building a better world. They must not be discouraged from aspiring toward greatness for they are to be the leaders of tomorrow.

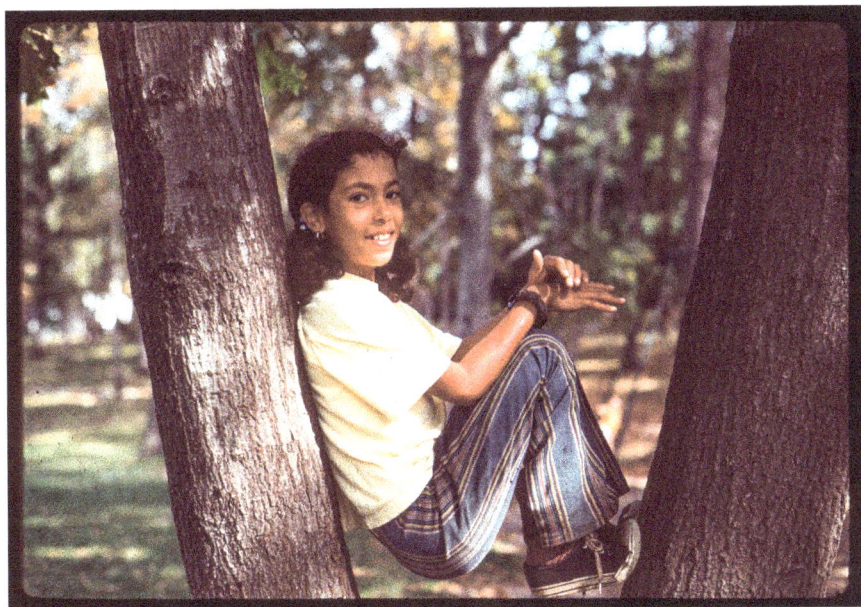

Photo courtesy of the Roberts Family

Introduction

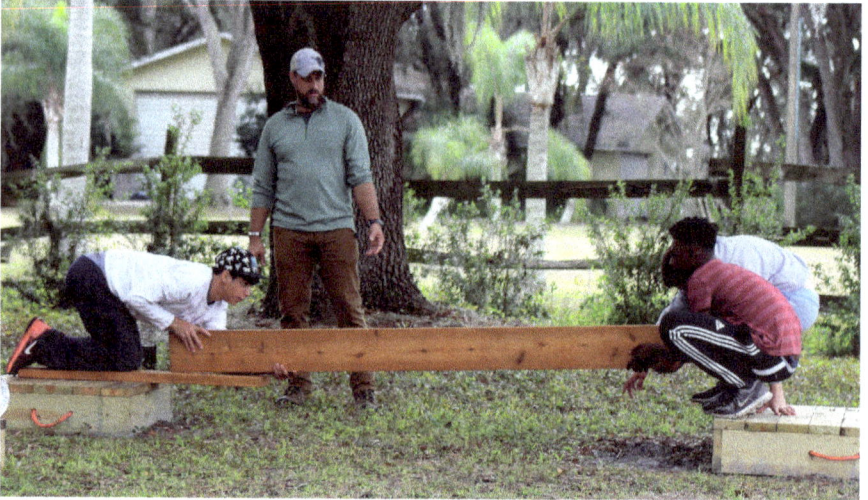

Photo courtesy of Sherry Bagley

Introduction

Sky Gray, Christine Norton, Rita Yerkes

In this field guide, readers find park rangers and experiential education leaders, practitioners, and researchers taking personal risks, challenging the status quo, laying tracks for change, and telling heartfelt stories from the field on diversity, equity, inclusion, and belonging (DEIB). Dr. Nina Roberts and Sky Gray shared DEIB work for over 25 years and had many heart-centered conversations about what could make the outdoors and programs more accessible. One tool they envisioned was a field guide for DEIB in the outdoors that leaders could use in the field, classroom, or boardroom.

Nina and Sky landed on this vision and began the work as two women cooking up some change, hope, and "good trouble." During the later stages of visioning the project, Nina's energy waned due to the progression of her cancer. They continued to meet and Nina identified colleagues to contribute to the guide and asked Sky to invite others to keep moving the vision forward, to identify gaps, and to address social justice challenges head on. In one of her last personal conversations with Sky, Sarita Gray, and Christine Norton, Nina asked that they pick up her torch and capture her social justice hopes and dreams in this project. Nina paved the way to invite those with shared passions to join in this quest and now her legacy, *DEIB Field Guide: Stories of Lived Experience.*

As a result, this field guide is filled with a diversity of change agents, poets, activists, social justice advocates, singers, drummers, young people, and wise sages sharing their personal reflections on DEIB. The field guide is a conversation starter, a source of inspiration, and a call to action. It is a bridge for leaders, practitioners, and researchers involved in experiential programs to gain an understanding of these authors' lived experiences and social justice challenges that have existed and still exist today.

In this field guide 40 authors reflect on their personal experiences with racism, sexism, heterosexism, gender identity, ableism, and ageism in the outdoors. These authors' reflections provide counterstorytelling or counternarratives to some of the common embedded practices in outdoor professions. They share DEIB topics and incidents that continue to challenge many leaders, practitioners, and researchers who use experiential education methodology.

Illuminating the stories of marginalized people can provide avenues to share "untold" experiences (Harper, 2009). Often these stories are counternarratives to the common deficit perspective about marginalized people. In contrast,

> counter-storytelling presents more authentic narratives about people of color [and other populations that have experienced oppression] that emanate directly from those within the community. This method allows for voices that are often unheard to be elevated,thereby presenting perspectives from within the community that are more balanced, insightful, and genuine. (Essien & Wood, 2021, p. 27)

This field guide does not address all situations and challenges that leaders, practitioners and researchers may encounter in advocating for DEIB, however it furthers the dialogue by bringing more voices to the outdoor experiential education community. Readers are challenged to dig deep, engage, and listen to the voices captured in this field guide with open hearts and minds to make personal and systemic program changes.

Exploring Pathways Toward Diversity, Equity, Inclusion, and Belonging

Exploring avenues toward DEIB can feel overwhelming in the face of insidious, systemic racial and social injustice, but we have role models and research to lead us forward. Dr. Nina believed that it is our moral and spiritual duty to move forward in this work, to break the silence, even when we are tired or afraid. Nina dedicated her life to removing barriers to access public lands and experiential programs, impacting multiple outdoor professions and their participants. Her advocacy and leadership inspired many people on this journey and continues today.

Nina's and Sky's goal for this field guide is to initiate courageous conversations that make experiential education leaders, practitioners, and researchers aware of DEIB issues and create more equity and access in the outdoors for their participants and themselves. Activist Audre Lorde (1977) said, "it is time to transform our silence into language and action." The contributors in this DEIB field guide attempt to do that, to use their voices to move outdoor professionals toward equitable actions. The stories shared in this field guide may elicit discomfort or even disbelief, and for those who have had similar experiences, these stories may bring up difficult memories or elicit anger—or perhaps validation. Some of the contributors to this guide expressed, "writing down painful memories is harder than I thought, yet important." Another author, referring to a youth BIPOC program, mentioned that "the program reviewers didn't think that a program like ours could achieve such positive data and reviewed us several times more than was typical."

A particular kind of empathy is required to move leaders, practitioners, and researchers towards greater social justice. Researchers call this social empathy, defined as "the ability to more deeply understand people by perceiving or experiencing their life situations and as a result gain insight into structural inequalities and disparities" (Segal, 2011, p. 266). This concept is not new and was introduced earlier by social activist Jane Addams, who believed that "in community and in groups, empathy and compassion could be introduced and strengthened for one another" (Malekoff & Papell, 2012, p. 310). By reading the authors' reflections and quotes in this field guide, readers are invited to develop a greater capacity for their own social empathy and commit to equitable practices such as:

♦ Engage in equity listening: Equity listening is a deep, non-defensive listening that aims to create trusting spaces for people to share experiences with oppression. Yancy (2020) encourages us to "Listen deeply to the plaintive calls for change" (para. 11) to combat the systemic, multi-tiered "isms" that exist in our world. Velasquez (2020) believes that this kind of deep listening can move us from defensiveness to openness, but that we need to create ecosystems where this kind of genuine listening can thrive.

♦ Create equity ecosystems: Consider the spaces in which we do our work. When we bring people together from different backgrounds take time to intentionally attend to their physical, social, spiritual, and psychological safety. Tools such as brave space agreements, group norms, and guidelines for courageous conversations can help create ecosystems or communities in which equity and empathy can thrive.

♦ Express empathy: The value of empathy is based on how it is expressed. Whether or not you have had a similar experience doesn't matter. You are not there to argue with someone else's reality, but rather hold space and honor the difficult and unique struggles of another person.

- Privilege: The concept of privilege is well-known through Peggy McIntosh's work on unpacking the invisible knapsack of white privilege (2007). However, the concept of privilege also applies to gender and gender identity, sexual orientation, ability, class, age, religion, and more. Ownership of privilege allows us to acknowledge that we benefit from privilege even if we are not actively trying to manipulate or exploit it to our advantage. Yet, our desire to be seen as allies can get in the way of owning our privilege because we want to defend our intent rather than looking at the impact our privilege has on others. However, "intent and impact are not the same thing. Good intentions do not mitigate negative effects" (Foster, 2004, p. 2).

- Consider the realities of intergenerational and complex trauma: DEIB work is systemic, historical, and intergenerational work. Black, Indigenous, People of Color (BIPOC) folx, women, Jewish people, LGBTQAI+ people, and others who have been historically marginalized, often experience the transmission of historical trauma, which includes racial and gender-based trauma, in which the cumulative effects of racism and sexism take a toll on an individual's mental and physical health (Isobel et al., 2019). This is also true for other "isms" and requires a broad commitment to systemic change versus relying solely on interpersonal solutions.

- Move past performative allyship: In the day and age of social media, it's easy to showcase one's values through memes, posts, and other social media commentary. The authors in this field guide encourage individuals and organizations to move past DEIB statements and into action that dismantles systemic barriers and addresses the need for power sharing and reparations. It challenges the reader to think less in terms of being allies and more in terms of being antioppressive co-

conspirators who speak truth to power and adopt antiracist and antisexist practices, which means "putting our privilege on the line for somebody" (Ekpe et al., 2022, p. 69).

Use the words of Audre Lorde (1977) to challenge and inspire as you read this field guide and do the work of DEIB:

> We can learn to work and speak when we are afraid in the same way we have learned to work and speak when we are tired. For we have been socialized to respect fear more than our own needs for language and definition, and while we wait in silence for that final luxury of fearlessness, the weight of that silence will choke us. The fact that we are here and that I speak these words is an attempt to break that silence and bridge some of those differences between us, for it is not difference which immobilizes us, but silence. And there are so many silences to be broken. (para. 12)

Nina left us way too soon. However, she left us with this inspiration,

> We must each learn to challenge systems, change institutional injustices, and more. We must all do our part to show up, speak up, and not tolerate hate and injustice. Be brave, be bold, be inspirational. Now is the time for new changes and transformation. In the process, reach deep down to share empathy, be patient with yourself and each other, and be authentic in your exchange of love, laughter, fear, and hope. (Roberts, 2022, p. 1)

References

Ekpe, L., & Toutant, S. (2022). Moving beyond performative allyship: A conceptual framework for anti-racist co-conspirators. In K. Johnson, N. Sparkman-Key, A. Meca, & S. Tarver (Eds.), *Developing anti-racist practices in the helping professions: Inclusive theory, pedagogy, and application* (67–93). Palgrave Macmillan.

Essien, I.R. & Wood, J.L. (2021). Do Black minds matter? Ascriptions of intelligence and the experiences of Black boys and girls in early childhood education. *Journal of the Alliance of Black School Educators, 11*(1), 21–41.

Foster, S. R. (2004). Causation in antidiscrimination law: Beyond intent versus impact. *Houston Law Review 41*, 1469.

Harper, S. R. (2009). Niggers no more: A critical race counternarrative on Black male student achievement at predominantly White colleges and universities. *International Journal of Qualitative Studies in Education*, *22*(6), 697–712.

Isobel, S., Goodyear, M., Furness, T., & Foster, K. (2019). Preventing intergenerational trauma transmission: A critical interpretive synthesis. *Journal of Clinical Nursing*, *28*(7–8), 1100–1113.

Lorde, A. (1977). The transformation of silence into language and action. In *Identity politics in the women's movement*, 81–84. https://wgs10016.commons.gc.cuny.edu/lorde-poetry-is-not-a-luxury/

Malekoff, A., & Papell, C. P. (2012). Remembering Hull House, speaking to Jane Addams, and preserving empathy. *Social Work with Groups*, *35*(4), 306–312.

McIntosh, P. (2007). White privilege: Unpacking the invisible knapsack. In P.S. Rothenberg (Ed.), *Race, Class, and Gender in the United States: An Integrated study* (177–182). Macmillan.

Roberts, N. (2022). Homepage Nina Roberts, Ph.D., Professor. https://ninaroberts-sfsu.com

Photo courtesy of the Roberts Family

Reflection Papers

Photo courtesy of Outward Bound Adventures

A Mirror and A Door

Carolyn Finney

I want to talk about the now and the stories we make. And the stories we tell. Especially as it relates to all things green. What does it look like to practice ruthlessness in our storytelling? What are the things we still don't, won't, and can't say about ourselves, about our country's past, and about our present? You know what I mean: that legacy of contradictions about who we are as a people on this land at this time. Indigenous removal and this land is your land; slavery and land of the free, home of the brave; the wall along our border with Mexico and "Give me your tired, your poor/ Your huddled masses." The list is long. It can get kind of funky when you start to pull back the curtain and really look. Andmake no mistake about it, the stories we tell and the narratives we perpetuate inform policy, shape public perception, color relationships, and determine direction for us all and the planet. Simply put, the stories we tell about who we are as a people and who we've been matter.

In 1999, I went to graduate school to work on my doctorate in geography. From 1999 until 2003, I didn't talk a lot about where I grew up in New York and how my parents were caretakers of a twelve-acre estate belonging to a wealthy White family. Instead, I was initially doing my dissertation on gender and conservation in Nepal. But in every class I took that focused on the environment (which was almost every class I took), I became slightly obsessed by two facts: I was almost always the only Black person in the room and there was rarely, if ever, any readings by or about Black people on any of the syllabi. I thought to myself, where the Black people at?

So, that first year of grad school I decided to write my end-of-the-year paper on making a case for a Black Feminist Political

Ecology, in large part because I was trying to find myself (and others who look like me) in the readings. Where was our agency? Where was our presence? Where was our voice? My advisor egged me on to do this for my dissertation while simultaneously explaining that no one there knew anything about this so while I would be supported, I would be taking this academic journey on my own. After a series of events outside of my control (9/11 and political unrest in Nepal), I decided to shift the focus of my research to African Americans and the environment in the United States. Needless to say, I was a bit overwhelmed; I was putting together a new proposal on something no one seemed to have written about before and the work suddenly felt so personal. It was at this point that I truly started looking for African Americans in the environmental literature, but I was always coming up wanting. I was not able to find anything on the library shelves, except the "bad things" that happen to Black people (such as slavery, redlining, and health-related effects of poor air quality).

How am I supposed to tell a story within an institutional set of expectations (being rigorous in my fact-finding) when my/our voice is absent? Where were the Black nature stories? What does it mean to be Black and to be green? That's when I had to get creative and began looking for our history, our memories, our visions for the future in poetry, art, music, oral history, and memoir. I had to draw outside the lines that were predetermined by a point of view that did not know how to see me and those who looked like me. This is also where I began looking at my own story.

In Maura Cheeks' (2021) article "Isn't Black Representation what we wanted?" in the Paris Review, Fran Lebowitz asks "why does everyone want to see themselves in books?" Lebowitz goes on to say that she doesn't understand people who complain about not seeing themselves in books. "A book is not supposed to be a mirror," she says, "it's supposed to be a door." Cheeks, who is

African American, writes, "I understand the sentiment, but I disagree with the argument. It's the type of sentiment that can only be felt by someone who was unknowingly represented almost everywhere she turned. She didn't know what she had." In another conversation with Lebowitz, the late African American writer Toni Morrison says, "I am the reader of the books I write." "Your other readers aren't you," Lebowitz pushes. And Morrison, laughing, replies, "Yes, they are."

I've been thinking about representation in terms of whose stories are centered, who is centered, how we all frame our understanding, and where our bias comes into play. I've been thinking about that when I think about folks like Henry David Thoreau and John Muir, whose voices and experiences have defined a set of practices and memories of who we are as human beings and as North Americans in relationship to non-human nature. I've been thinking about how our collective experience in the environment has been defined by individuals who don't look like me and, for all their good intentions, miss the complexity and their complicity embedded in their assumption that we all have access to a nature that they've defined in their own image.

In 2021, the *NY Times* asked me to write a piece for their series, "Black History, continued," where I explored the idea of a Black environmental imaginary. Along with sharing stories of Black folks past and present, who have always been on the landscape, I talked about my five years backpacking around the world and never seeing anyone who looked like me. The editors asked me how these stories had inspired me to begin doing this work. But they didn't understand. I was inspired to do this work because I was tired of being relegated to the sidelines of a story that didn't know how to see me. And I knew the stories were out there because I was out there.

My decision to include my environmental story in my work helped me be transparent and situated while revealing my bias, perspective, and history in the shadow of a dominant environmental narrative that rarely considered the experience or presence of anyone who looked like me. Telling my story in relationship to others clarifies where I stand and who I stand with, authentically and honestly. It is a choice I make, rigorously and ruthlessly. And it is an invitation for others to do the same. Everyone has a story and for those of us whose stories have been erased, ignored, and unconsidered, it means that we can make the choice to tell our story, regardless.

There isn't a script for this moment—we get to write it. We get to write what "justice" is—we aren't simply observers or background actors. I've often heard the statement, "Change the narrative." Well, we are the narrative. We are the story, which implies accountability, responsibility, and possibility. We can make change, one story at a time.

References

Cheeks, M. (2021). Isn't Black representation what we wanted? *Paris Review, 12*(6), 88–94.

Finney, C. (2021, November 4). Who gets left out of the great outdoors story? *The NY Times.* https://www.nytimes.com/2021/11/04/style/black-outdoors-wilderness.html

The Association for Experiential Education's Evolving Journey Toward Diversity, Equity, Inclusion, and Belonging

Rita Yerkes

In 1980, I attended my first Association for Experiential Education (AEE) Conference. The conference was filled with amazing people and sessions. I thought that I had found my professional home. Excited and holding my new AEE membership card in hand, I went to my first Annual Membership Meeting. After Boardintroductions and announcements, the treasurer gave his report ending with the statement that the organization had major financial challenges ahead. The Board chair then asked if there were any questions. I raised my hand and asked, "how did this happen?" Silence filled the auditorium. The chair then asked me, "are you a member?" I said, "yes," but he did not answer my question. I left the meeting disturbed. Instead of finding my new professional home, I felt that I was not valued as a participating member. At that moment, AEE did not appear to value diversity, equity, inclusion, or belonging.

Questioning—Men's and Women's Interests Group

After much reflection, I decided to renew my AEE membership and attended the next conference. I joined Men's and Women's Special Interest Group and noticed the meetings attendance was by 98% women and 2% men. Most of the discussions centered around women's issues in experiential education programs and with AEE. Women found themselves as the minority in their own programs and were paid less. They struggled with how to advance their careers and feared their voices were not welcome by their employers and AEE. One example was the decision to hold the AEE conference in Missouri when that state had voted down the Equal Rights Amendment (ERA); as a result, the women members boycotted the conference that year. Men on the other end of the spectrum had few issues to discuss.

Women's Special Interest Group

After several years convening the Men's and Women's Special Interest Group, women at the 1985 Colorado AEE Conference voted to change the group name to the Women's Special Interest Group due to the lack of participation by men. This group wanted to address the many issues of diversity, equity, inclusion, and belonging in AEE and experiential education organizations. These issues included women having a place at the AEE Boardtable, lack of women published in AEE publications, lack of women on key AEE committees, and lack of women chosen as workshop leaders and keynote speakers.

Leadership and Persistence

What followed was a classic lesson in diversity, equity, inclusion, and belonging. Members joined the AEE Women's Special Interest Group from all over the USA and other countries and set to work. Facilitated by Linda Cooper, Chris Heeter, Lee Lovinfosse, Mary McClintock, Denise Mitten, Wilma Miranda, Judith Niemi, Jean Vrbka, Karen Warren, and Rita Yerkes, the group brought women's issues to the AEE Board's and members' attention. This group of extraordinary women and many allies strove to give women a voice in AEE. They mentored women at AEE conferences by giving workshops, co-presenting, co-authoring, serving on conference and board committees to identify women speakers and consultants, and guest editing and serving on the *Journal of Experiential Education* advisory committee (Yerkes, 1997).

In 1987, the group became the Women's Professional Group (WPG) and advocated that AEE become a more diverse organization. They proposed the first AEE Statement of Diversity, which was adopted by the Board. They proposed AEE diversity initiatives to provide a more inclusive atmosphere at AEE conferences. They conducted fundraisers so that members of lower income could attend conferences (Yerkes, 1997). They supported social justice projects such as "Take Back the Trails,"led by Nina Roberts, and the publication of the book *Women's Voices in Experiential Education*, edited by Karen Warren. The WPG led and became a model for groups forming within AEE such as NAALA (Natives, Africans, Asians, Latinos & Allies), LGBA (Lesbian, Gays, Bisexuals & Allies), and others (Garvey, et al., 2008).

Diversity, Equity, Inclusion, and Belonging Lessons Learned

The WPG provided women and men an amazing and shared journey in challenging an organization to listen, respond, and invite others to join. Through its inclusive style and initiatives, it made AEE, experiential education, and the world a better place.

That Was Then, But This Is Now

Given the state of the world in 2022, we seem to have to redo all that we have achieved over the years when it comes to diversity, equity, inclusion, and belonging. DEIB is a continual process and can be overshadowed due to other individual and organizational demands. As Nina Roberts said passionately,

> we and our outdoor and experiential education organizations must continue to listen, educate, and move forward; we must work hard and continue to affect sustained social justice change so that all are welcomed, represented and have a place at the table. (N. Roberts, personal communication, September 23, 2021)

Following her example, consider these points:

- Always know your voice is important and that you have something to contribute!

- Self-evaluate, listen, learn, and both share with and mentor others.

- If you are not able to be at the table, recruit and support someone who will attend and represent your interests, issues, and possible solutions.

- Always know that you are not alone—educate, cultivate allies, create, and be patient.

- Support and hold organizations like AEE accountable, who have diversity, equity, inclusion, and belonging in their mission, to constantly revisit their policies and practices to see if they are meeting these goals through measurable actions.

References

Garvey, D., Mitten, D., Pace, S. & Roberts, N., 2008. History of the Association of Experiential Education. In K. Warren, D. Mitten, & T. Loeffler (Eds.), *Theory & Practice of Experiential Education*, 1st ed. Association of Experiential Education, pp. 98–99.

Yerkes, R., 1997. How it all began: An overview. In N. Roberts (Ed.), *Women in Experiential Education Professional Group: A Collective Account of Our Roots and Growth*, 1st ed. Association of Experiential Education, pp. 2–3.

Photo courtesy of Rita Yerkes

The Picnic Table at the 1983 AEE Conference

Karen Warren

Let me tell you a story that starts with driving across country from Massachusetts to Lake Geneva, Wisconsin, with eight of my Experiential Education class students to attend our first AEE conference. It was 1983, my first semester teaching at Hampshire College. There's something crazy about driving 22 hours each way for a weekend conference. But I had convinced the students we would get something out of it.

And we did. The students reveled in the excitement of finally having words that supported their cherished vision of what education should be. They enthusiastically shared new skills and ideas from workshops. They spoke of the interesting, passionate educators they met.

My own takeaways were both similar and profoundly different. I, too, was totally pumped by the new ideas and the people I met at the conference. However, my main transformative moment happened late at night at an isolated picnic table beside Lake Geneva.

It started that morning in the women's bathroom at the conference site. There was a note inside that asked if there wereany lesbians in outdoor education, and if so, come meet at the picnic table by the lake after the keynote speaker that night.

I saw the note several times that day and my internal anxiety continued to rise each time. I had already spent almost a decade as a closeted lesbian in the outdoor fields. I wanted to meet others like me, but I was terrified. What if someone found out about me? What if one of my students was at the picnic table? Would I hate myself if I was not brave enough to go?

Remember, these were different times in the world and the outdoor adventure fields. Teachers wore paper bags over their heads as they marched in Pride parades so they wouldn't be fired. Lesbian role models just didn't exist for me in my small-town Midwestern upbringing. Lessons in internalized homophobia were well taught in school and at home.

In outdoor programs, women instructors were told not to mention women partners for fear it would get back to parents and jeopardize recruitment of students. Lesbian baiting was rampant (McClintock, 1996). It wasn't unusual for out lesbians or those suspected of being lesbians to be silenced or fired.

This very real fear swirled through my head as I filed into the keynote speech. I didn't know if I was going to the picnic table or not. I didn't know if I could step around that fear. And I wonderedif I would regret not going.

I tried to focus on the keynote speaker to calm my mind. The speaker was a well-respected and renowned leader in the outdoor adventure education world. I was excited to hear his wisdom. Yet, as I listened, my feelings became more muddled.

He started his speech with a lengthy list of people who have been important to him in his career. For each one he had an entertaining story about their relationship. As he went on from one name to the next, I thought to myself, these are all men. Where are the women in outdoor experiential education? Finally,at the end of the long accolades, he ended by thanking his secretary. However, he didn't mention her name. She was the tireless secretary with no name.

As I sat there taken aback by this silence about women, I knewat that minute I needed to be at the picnic table by the lake. I didn't stay until the end of the keynote. The floor length windows were open to let in the breeze, so I jumped out of the window into the darkness. I took a few deep breaths, hoped my students were anywhere but at the picnic table, and headed off into the woods by the lake.

There were six of us at that picnic table. There were women who would become my friends and mentors as I negotiated the next 40 or so years of my involvement with AEE. I don't particularly remember what was said that night. It really didn't matter. What mattered was that we showed up as our true selves. I had the almost giddy feeling of power that comes with authenticity.

Lessons From the Picnic Table

If a meeting in the dark woods can be a call for change, this moment certainly was. Women in AEE could see that our jobwas to amplify the voices of women and girls in experiential education. We found that speaking truth to power was accomplished most effectively by joining together.

We mentored women to take leadership roles in AEE and to get published in the *Journal of Experiential Education* and other publications. The Women's Professional Group became a forum to voice the needs and concerns of women in AEE and the larger professional community. It was also a safe space to connect with other women and non-binary colleagues.

When Colorado enacted an amendment in 1992 that repealed existing state laws protecting lesbians, gay men, and bisexuals from discrimination, the LGBT interest group of AEE formed. Since AEE had its office and conference in Colorado that year, hard choices about how to respond to this oppressive amendment brought dialogue about LGBTQ+ people in AEE into focus.

The foremost lesson was that the marginalization of one group of people is tightly connected to the experiences of all oppressed people. Intersectionality shows that different forms of oppression intersect, overlap, and amplify discrimination. Racism, sexism, classism, heterosexism and homophobia, transphobia, ableism, ageism, and religious oppression still exist in outdoor and experiential education programs and practice (Warren et al., 2014).

Have times changed since the picnic table meeting next to Lake Geneva? In some ways, yes. I don't see many paper bags now at Pride Marches. I can be an out educator and focus on teaching to transgress (hooks, 1994) without sanction. There areadvocates and allies in AEE speaking up for social justice.

Yet, unfortunately, the rights and respect for marginalized people are continually under attack. The outdoor and experiential education fields are not exceptions. Are marginalized people as equally represented at the boardroom tables as we have been at the picnic tables? Are microaggressions the new replacement for obvious acts of discrimination in our programs? Are we willing to interrogate our individualistic, risk-loving, wilderness-centered notions of "real" outdoor adventure? Can we move beyond the image of a homogenous, ideal outdoor leader (Rao & Roberts, 2018)?

Transformations require action. They take collective voices continuing to ask hard questions and interrupt silence. They take moving past fear to a promise of justice.

Nina Roberts raised her voice with others in pursuit of social justice. She worked tirelessly, risked censure when she spoke out, and asked us all to be on the path to diversity, equity,inclusion, and belonging with her.

I leave you with a question. Who will fill Nina's shoes, if not you?

References

hooks, b. (1994). *Teaching to transgress: Education as the practice of freedom.* Routledge.

McClintock, M. (1996). Lesbian baiting hurts all women. In K. Warren (Ed.), *Women's voices in experiential education* (pp. 241–250). Kendall/ Hunt.

Rao, T. & Roberts, N.S. (2018). Voices of women of color: Dreaming of an inclusive outdoor leadership environment. In T. Gray & D. Mitten (Eds.) *The Palgrave international handbook of women and outdoor learning* (pp. 815–835). Palgrave Macmillan.

Warren, K., Roberts, N.S., Breunig, M., & Alvarez, M.A. (2014). Social justice in outdoor experiential education: A state of knowledge review. *Journal of Experiential Education, 37*(1), 89–103. https://doi.org/ 10.1177/1053825913518898

Photo courtesy of Robbie Francis

The Road to Justice is Long

Karla Henderson and Deb Bialeschki

We have experienced a long road as we reflect on our careers addressing equity, justice, diversity, inclusion, and belonging. We do not see the end in sight. We are, however, grateful for the contributions we have made along with others who have included their stories in this book.

For more than 40 years, our personal lives and professional work have focused on bringing visibility to groups discounted by a White patriarchy. Our mission has been primarily to highlight women's lives related to leisure and the outdoors through research, teaching, and practice. An initial focus on women led to recognizing that huge differences exist among women and girls. We sought to create a foundation to better understand and appreciate the contributions that all women and girls make to society, which have implications for other markers of identity.

Our work and the work of other like-minded professionals have created a tapestry woven by the threads of diversity, equity, inclusion, and justice. Our experiences provide the basis for three lessons we have learned along our journey: collaboration, persistence, and evolution toward social action. These reflections may be informative to others who value justice work.

Collaboration is Key

We acknowledge the importance of the stories of people who came before us whether they were students, research interviewees, or colleagues. Many people opened doors and shattered ceilings to bring awareness to inequities, stereotypes, and social mores. The collective impact within this movement has been far greater than isolated individual efforts.

An example of the outcomes of collaboration happened in 1981 when we offered the first class focusing on women and leisure at the University of Wisconsin-Madison. Karla was the instructor and Deb was a PhD student. Several graduate students had taken a class on the philosophy of leisure and were outraged that none of the assigned readings were written by women, and the discussion of women was non-existent. They wanted a classthat made women the center of the discourse. This class began our search to include women in the leisure and outdoor curriculaas well as in the research literature. Deb wrote one of the first dissertations on women's leisure and later proposed a cross-listed leisure/women's studies course when she began her academic appointment at the University of North Carolina at Chapel Hill in 1985.

During the 1980s, other progressive individuals in the United States and Canada such as Sue Shaw, Diane Samdahl, Nina Roberts, Denise Mitten, Rita Yerkes, and Karen Warren to mention only a few, were committed to diversity. The Association for Experiential Education started a women's interest professional group. An online women's listserv was established to share research and ideas. The World Leisure Organization instituted a task force that later became a Commission on Women and Leisure. Young scholars emerged expanding the research on the experiences of women and providing opportunities to collaborate on examining gender intersections with aspects such as race, ethnicity, and sexual orientation.

We are proud to continue to be part of a committed and growing group of professionals who understand that none of us are free until all of us are free. Justice cannot be denied when a passionate, committed group of individuals come together as one to confront invisibility, stigma, prejudice, and inequities. The circle of collaborators continues to grow due to the persistence embodied over decades.

Persistence Pays Off

Persistence is necessary to accomplish any worthwhile goal. Early in our careers, we believed that the leisure and outdoor fields could do better relative to inclusion and justice. We did not falter in the commitment to bring visibility to women's lived experiences—not as a comparison or complement to men but asan affirming and visible story about women in all parts of their lives.

Convincing gatekeepers of scholarly journals to accept feminist research and research by, for, and about women as legitimate scholarship was an on-going struggle early in our careers. Collaboration enabled us to persist. Coworkers were instrumental in applauding our work, providing constructive critiques, offering useful edits, and cheering us on as well asoccasionally affording a shoulder for crying.

The important lesson for us was to keep going and not give up. It was not easy. We knew the road would be long and winding. We did our best and are grateful that others continue to persist in addressing women's issues and the complexities of equity and diversity in society. This work includes research and teaching as well as ways to convert information into action.

Evolution Toward Social Action

Rhetoric and research without action does not change the world. Translating information to practice and community activism are necessary for social change. An example of an action taken to raise awareness of social injustice was our involvement in the Society of Park and Recreation Educators Teaching Symposiumin 1990 that focused on social responsibility. The idea of social responsibility necessitated addressing inclusion, social justice, and environmental sustainability. We challenged participants toleave the symposium with a commitment to move classroom ideas into community action focused on social justice.

An understanding of women's leisure as well as other issues of diversity has evolved over our careers. Terminology has changed markedly although the intent of the efforts has remained focused on justice. Some early work was incomplete and sophomoric by today's understanding. For example, in 1989we proposed a general education perspectives course entitled Leisure and Diversity. At its fundamental level, it was about drawing awareness to diverse groups and how they might experience leisure based on gender, race, ability, income status,religion, and sexual orientation. Classes now exist in higher education with a more sophisticated analysis of inequity and inclusion that also examine the social construction of diversity.

The evolving study of women and equity has taken an ecological perspective. Our early focus was on individuals. Today, the issues of social constructions and other philosophical frameworks have progressed to rigorous analyses that go beyond simple conclusions toward explaining emerging contradictions. Analyses include individuals as well as their relationships with others, local communities, legislation and policies, and societal attitudes and pressures.

The initial foundation was necessary so that a plethora of current topics and analyses could evolve toward 21st century issues. Current research builds on previous assertions, challenges them, and adds to the discourse with new explanations. This evolution is necessary and welcomed.

Parting Thoughts

We believe our career efforts provided a foundation for the greater good as we offered a consistent goal of equity and justice.

Dynamic new scholarship and action move all journeys further down the road. Human beings do the best they can with what they have in the moment. Many individuals are now on this long road to justice and this book is an attestation to those ongoing commitments.

We are grateful for colleagues like Nina Roberts who listened and wove more threads into the tapestry of diversity, equity, belonging, and justice. Inclusive stories shared through lenses of gender, race, ethnicity, ability, identity, and other social constructions are necessary. A book such as this one would not have been possible 40 years ago. With gratitude, we contribute a small piece to this expanding body of influence that continues to shine a light on the road to justice for all.

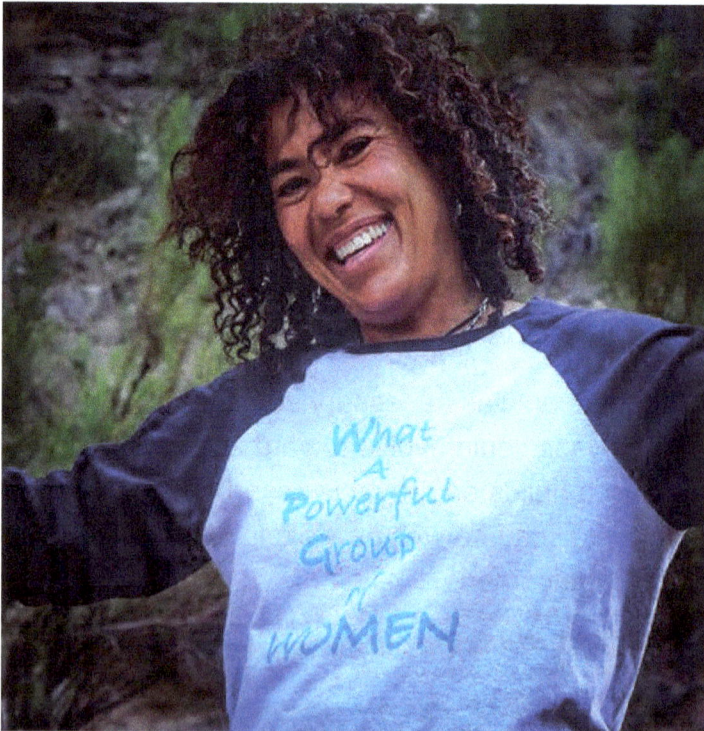

Photo courtesy of Sharon Washington

Viewed as An Alien: Race-based Assumptions in the Outdoors

Sharon J. Washington

I love being outside in beautiful remote places where the noise of society fades away and the sound of an airplane far overhead stands out as a reminder of civilization. Spending time camping was a way for our family to travel before public accommodations were welcoming to Blacks. My dad nurtured my love for the outdoors, and participating in Girl Scouts provided opportunities for me to learn essential outdoor and leadership skills.

Simultaneously, I was learning valuable lessons of self-worth and cultural pride from my family and from the countless Black elders in my life. These lessons over time would forge an internal resiliency strong enough to buffer me from the impact of the daily onslaught of systemic racism I encountered. The interaction of the two forces forged an internal resiliency that would sustain me throughout my life.

Three early lessons stand out in my memory. The first two were taught before I began school and were reinforced often. The third one was taught when I was in elementary school, although I didn't really come to understand it until I was in college and beyond. The first was delivered by my big brother in a call and response cadence: I am - somebody, I am - gifted, I am - beautiful! For the second lesson, my mom instructed me and my sister that if our White teachers (and they were all White) told us something about what we could or could not do or achieve and it differed from what we heard at home, we were to ignore them. Third, and repeatedly, my mom would say "people teach you how to treat them." Over time I became an astute scholar of human behavior and would notice how their words at times weredifferent from their actions. These three lessons and more helped me navigate the assumptions of White people who questioned my legitimacy in what I refer to as the assumption that I as a Black person was an alien in the outdoors. This assumption by many White people asserts that Black folks are not drawn to, comfortable in, knowledgeable about, or have experience in a range of spaces beyond the stereotypes and depictions promulgated in television, movies, advertisements, schools, etc. The constant and ongoing assumption is that I, as aBlack woman, am an alien in outdoor spaces.

It was 1970, the summer between 4th and 5th grade. My sister and I were playing in the swimming pool of the apartment complex where we lived when a White man began questioning us as to whether we were guests of someone who lived at the complex. When he learned we lived at the complex, he then questioned us on how we learned to swim and asked where we were from since we didn't speak like any Black people he knew. Iremember at the time I thought he was a little stupid for asking us how we learned to swim, since we learned, like everyone else, from somebody who knew how to swim. In our case, it was our dad. The questions about where we were from and how we spoke rattled me since everyone in our family spoke the same way and we were all from Columbus, Ohio. When we got home, Iremember asking mom why we talked differently from other Black people. Of course, she wanted to know what prompted myquestions. But more disturbing, as I reflect on the experience, is that my nearly 10-year-old self didn't question the White man's knowledge of "how Black people speak," and how his limited knowledge was likely based on stereotypes and little to no direct experience with Black people.

It's familiar and exhausting to be the recipient of White people's projected bias about Black folks. Whether I'm riding a chair lift, resting on the side of a trail, or rafting on a river, I'm questioned about "how I got there." I'm not asked how's the snow, how's my day going, or anything else about the actual experience. It's as though their expectation is that I accidentally found myself outdoors. The following experience provides an example of how one might acknowledge the reality of outdoor expertise when a previous assumption was incorrect.

In March 2022, I was on a horseback riding excursion in Patagonia with seven White women from the United States, our two White Chilean guides, and our head gaucho, who was a mixed-race Chilean man. The guides and the head gaucho greeted each other and then welcomed our group to the estancia. We were instructed to put on a pair of chaps to protect our calves after which the head gaucho looked the group over and assigned us to horses based on his assumptive assessment. I was the last chosen and given the smallest horse.Once the ride began, I realized it differed from trail rides in the States where the horses docilly follow each other never straying from the line and resistant to cues from the riders. Within severalminutes the horse I was riding was responding to weight changes for stopping, starting, and the desired pace, so there was little need to use the reins. Approximately a third of the way into the ride the head gaucho stopped and motioned for one of the women to get off her horse. He then turned to me and indicated that I should get off the horse I was riding. The guide translated that the gaucho didn't think she could control the horse and thought I would do better.

If that moment had been a cartoon, it would have been funny to see a large timer counting down in the upper corner of the screen while the guide was figuring out what to say next—five, four, three, two . . . "Sharon, how did you learn to ride? How longhave you been riding?" Blah, blah, blah. The questions themselves are loaded with assumptions about what non-Black people often have regarding what Black people can and cannot do, followed by them asking the Black person to legitimize how they gained a particular skill as though it was obtained illegally. Proving that I belong in the outdoors or any setting where I don't live down to a White person's expectations or assumptions of me is exhausting. This is why at the end of the ride, after I had dismounted and had taken off the chaps, the head gaucho looked me in the eye and said, "Eres muy buen jinete" (You're a very good horse rider). What a relief to be acknowledged without question.

Discussion Questions

- Describe a time when someone made an assumption about you while you were engaged in an outdoor activity. What was the assumption? If you could go back to that time, what would you like to have done differently or had someone else do differently?

- Describe a time when you made an assumption about someone else while they were engaging in an outdoor activity or something else that surprised you. What was the assumption? Who was the assumption about? If you could go back to that time, what, if anything, would you like to do differently?

- Are there instances or times when you felt someone viewed you as an alien in outdoor spaces? What did it feel like?

- What might be the basis for assumptions about who belongs outdoors and/or assumptions in general?

Photo courtesy of Sky Gray

Diversity Awareness as a Mindset: Doing What We Can Where We Can

Susie Barr-Wilson

I offer my reflections as a White woman in the outdoor recreation profession.

In fall 2008, I was halfway through my Peace Corps service and determined my next goal was to pursue a master's degree focused on empowering girls through outdoor recreation. Professors across the United States recommended I study with Dr. Nina Roberts at San Francisco State University (SFSU). They attested that she was the best of the best! Dr. Nina was indeed an amazing professor, helping craft my degree to focus on effective outdoor programming for adolescent girls, but her guidance didn't stop there. In her individual mentorship as well as in every one of her university classes, Dr. Nina challenged students to consider how to provide recreation opportunities for underrepresented populations, especially People of Color (POC). She emphasized the need to involve members of the community that we wish to serve on our leadership boards and planning teams. We discussed the importance of representation in marketing and having POC involved at every level of our organizations, from instructors to program managers to executive directors. I enrolled at SFSU thinking I would learn how to empower girls through outdoor adventure education, but I grew the most in diversity awareness, exploring inequities, and how to effectively include and support POC in outdoor programs.

Fast forward four years after graduating, I took an administrative position with a technical climbing/mountaineering school and guide services company in July 2016. Most of the clients and instructors were young, able-bodied, affluent White males.

Inspired by my graduate classes and conversations with Dr. Nina, I was motivated to "rock the boat" and challenge the way things had always been done in hopes of increasing justice, equity, diversity, and inclusion (JEDI) awareness. For this reflection, JEDI is used to refer to diversity and inclusion efforts in the same way that diversity, equity, and inclusion (DEI) or diversity, equity, inclusion, and belonging (DEIB) could be used. The following tips are drawn from my reflections working with this company, offered here as potential strategies for outdoor practitioners who find themselves in similar situations.

Tip #1: Challenge the status quo. Approximately six months after being hired, I approached the company president and cofounder, an older White affluent male, and recommended he hire a diversity and inclusion manager to support the organization in employing and serving more women and POC in their climbing programs. I was met with hesitancy and genuine surprise; the company was formed in the 1970s and this was seemingly the first time the issue of diversity in participation and staffing had been raised. The president requested time to think and asked me to research JEDI efforts in similar organizations before our next meeting.

Tip #2: Talk to others. While gathering examples of outdoor organizations that had established JEDI coordinators/programs, I spoke with other administrative staff at the company. The director of operations, also a White male, fully agreed that they were behind in diversity and inclusion efforts and committed to advocating for organizational change. Identifying this ally, someone who had worked for the company for many years, was immensely helpful in advancing the company's JEDI efforts. I reached out to Dr. Nina, and, per her suggestion, developed a one-page proposal outlining possible areas of JEDI work needed at the organization, including reviewing relevant articles and documentaries on trending issues, arranging diversity awareness trainings for guides and staff, updating the website and marketing materials to reflect more women and POC, andresearching possible partnerships with underrepresented populations.

Tip #3: Keep at it. I presented my proposal to the president in April 2017, and with the support of the director of operations, I was approved to work 3–4 hours/week as the diversity and inclusion coordinator. The president indicated that he wanted to focus on bringing in underrepresented populations (e.g., through marketing and recruitment) rather than on internal changes (e.g.,staff trainings). I respectfully stressed that both were necessary and that change needed to start from within. This includes education and support from the organization's leadership.

Tip #4: Watch for the opportunity. My first year as the diversity and inclusion coordinator involved significant research and consultations with JEDI leaders in the field, including Dr. Nina, the Avarna Group, Tanya Rao, and Miho Aida. I worked with the marketing director to design a webpage for the Women's Programs, compiled a Diversity and Inclusion Resource Manual, and I drafted three JEDI training modules. I recommended several staff trainings by professional JEDI facilitators.

Unfortunately, each staff training recommendation was met with resistance (e.g., "that consultant is too expensive," "it's really difficult to get our instructors to sit through trainings that long," and "that location is too far away"). This was frustrating and discouraging, but things quickly changed when the organization received a new Denali National Park permit that *required* guide service companies to provide staff training on diversity awareness. Ah, ha! The park permit requirement was the motivation necessary to proceed. The president approved me arranging the company's first "Diversity and Bias Awareness Training" in July 2018 that was presented by a cultural competency educator from the local Peace and Justice Center. For guides and office staff unable to attend, I created an asynchronous training on unconscious bias, JEDI vocabulary, and diversity issues in the field of outdoor recreation.

Shortly after the first staff training, I offered a virtual training for women guides and staff that highlighted women leaders in mountaineering, discussed inclusive approaches to outdoor programming, and allowed space for women guides and staff to share their personal challenges and successes as well as offer recommendations to the organization. Participants requested more frequent all-women's staff trainings and suggested that the company require gender awareness trainings for all guides. I shared this feedback with the director of operations. He was receptive and appreciative of the requests for additional trainings but did not take immediate action. In addition to staff trainings, I recommend outdoor companies provide regular affinity spaces for women and POC staff as well as ongoing diversity awareness trainings, as opposed to meeting one "check the box" requirement.

I moved onto other adventures in 2019, and I am happy to report that there is still a JEDI coordinator at the company, the webpage for the Women's Programs remains active, and in recent years they have partnered with organizations such as Latino Outdoors and Climbing for Change. In late 2020, the director of operations shared, "I'm really proud of what we're doing with DEI [JEDI] work . . . I can't tell you how much you inspired me to focus on this." I was glad to be in the right place at the right time to help the organization take steps towards more diversity and inclusion.

In closing, I recommend outdoor practitioners and companies wishing to expand their JEDI efforts start by having conversations with their organization's leadership (e.g., executive director, president, manager, board of directors). These key stakeholders need to be involved and on board with the importance of diversity awareness and increasing access to participation. Come to the table with specific ideas and examples of how similar organizations have adopted JEDI strategies. After your top leadership team is invested, consider these recommendations:

♦ Consult with experts in the field, professional JEDI educators and outdoor program advisors (e.g., Institute for Outdoor Learning, Miho Aida, Rue Mapp, The Avarna Group). Explore how your organization could partner with them to arrange staff trainings, recruit and hire POC staff, establish affinity spaces for POC staff, effectively market programs to underrepresented communities, and design programs to be more welcoming and supportive of POC participants.

♦ Recommend diversity trainings for staff at all levels of your organization, from the seasonal instructor and part-time administrative assistant to the president and director of programs and operations. Look into the resources available in your local community! Many cities and counties across the United States have Peace & Justice Centers; they might not offer outdoor-specific resources or trainings, but they might connect you with local organizations that focus on human rights.

♦ After following up with management once the conversations have started, be persistent. Organizational change is often slow and requires passion and dedication to move forward! Stay alert and watch for openings to advance JEDI efforts. Timing is everything; if your company is exploring a possible grant, permit, partnership, or marketing strategy that includes a JEDI component, this could be a key inroad for making larger organizational progress. Take advantage of the opportunity! When JEDI topics come up, ask how else the company can adopt and expand these efforts to move farther down the path towards social justice transformation in the outdoor industry.

Dedication: This reflection is dedicated to Dr. Nina Roberts, my former professor, advisor, and beloved mentor. I am grateful for Dr. Nina's candidness, for her guidance to think critically about equity and representation, and for her motivation to have the courage to act. Dr. Nina will forever inspire me and so many others to be our best selves. Let us carry her torch forward, doing what we can where we can to pave the way for increasing diversity and belonging in the outdoors.

Photo courtesy of AEE

From Urban Spaces to Wild Places: 45 years of Connecting Youth of Color to Natural Landscapes

Charles Thomas

For much of its history, environmental, conservation, and federal land management agencies have operated very much like a relaxed apartheid system. An "apartheid light," so to speak: a land use system that was segregated not so much by race, but by access; a system that discriminated by opportunity and was maintained, not so much by policy, but by privilege and cultural ascendancy. This system was created and forged in the fires of the American history of illegal land acquisition, exclusive land use, and blatant disregard for the inherent land rights and culture of those who were here long before Europeans arrived as well as a systematic exclusion of those who worked so hard to make the land profitable for colonial White America.

The dominant Euro-culture built a land ownership, use, and control empire and assigned themselves the job of guardians. This sense of guardianship has been passed down through generations, restricting access, opportunity, knowledge, and privilege to recreate in the outdoors. Whites have developed a pathway to an outdoor pedigree and made it difficult for people ofcolor to acquire that same pedigree.

Many people will find it difficult to fathom my assertion of apartheid light or draw from American history to explain why ethnic minorities have greatly increased in numbers yet are still so scarce in certain outdoor spaces today. They should bear inmind that it doesn't take an active group of practicing White Supremacists to maintain a White Supremacist's system or culture of exclusion. A culture of exclusion can easily be maintained by enlightened, well-intentioned people who are not White Supremacist but continue to operate within a system designed by and for White Supremacists.

Over the past 40 years, our environmental leaders have done an amazing job at saving our natural landscapes and recently have aggressively pursued an agenda that promotes diversity, equity, and inclusion. Still, many failed to see how they were complicit in perpetuating the lack of diversity. They established their hiring practices by promoting from within, by maintaining little to no relationships with diverse partners, and by committing to diversity initiatives without receiving feedback or input from the audiences they wished to involve. These practices have continued to contribute to their challenges attracting staff and participants to their programs.

Outdoor organizations might start solving these challenges by looking within. In a talk about leadership, Simon Sinek posited that the leaders in charge of removing the problem are indeed the problem, concluding that these leaders looked everywhere for the genesis of the problem except at themselves:

> You must take accountability for your actions. You can take all the credit inthe world for the things that you do right as long as you also takeresponsibility for the things you do wrong; it must be a balanced equation—you don't get it one way and not the other.

A multitude of institutional policies and historical events have kept members of urban communities of color away from the outdoors. Many have promoted and sustained outdoor recreation in White communities, who are the vast majority of outdoor users. Naturally, this creates the perception held by the mainstream outdoor users that Black, Indigenous, and People of Color (BIPOC) eschew the great outdoors. Over time, this has often led to stereotyped images and intentional and unintentional discriminatory behavior from the mainstream when they encounter BIPOC individuals outdoors. I have a vivid memory that occurred during a rafting trip that was instrumental in shaping my experience of being an "outdoor anomaly." Early in my career as a wilderness instructor at Outward Bound Adventures (OBA) (not to be confused with the National Outward Bound), I led a rafting trip in Northern California. As our group paddled the river in four eight-person rafts, each filled with Black, Brown, Indigenous, and Asian participants, we noticed spectators pointing and laughing at us on a bridge that arched across the river. Just as we went under the bridge one of the spectators yelled out, "Hey, did you guys just escape from prison?" We knew had we fit the profile of all the other rafters on the river that question would have never been asked. However, I guess in some form of poetic justice, 25 years later one of the oldest rafting organizations in California hired two OBA participants as their first African American river guides.

In the not-so-distant past on a beautiful bright June morning, I was leading a regular one-day course into a local wilderness area. We pulled our van up to a ranger's kiosk and I stepped out to ask the ranger directions to a specific trailhead. As I spoke to him, he looked past me and fixed his eyes on our group in the van, African Americans from South Los Angeles. I shared with him the trailhead I was interested in. Without inquiring about our experience level, he immediately stated, "You probably don't want to use that trail, it's very strenuous." I responded, "Great! That's exactly what we want." He diplomatically tried to dissuade me again by asking me if our kids were ready to do such a hike and did we have enough water with us. I assured him we did and then stepped aside to view a map and allow a family of four to approach the ranger with their questions. I overheard the father of the family ask the ranger for a moderately strenuous and fun hiking trail for him, his wife, and two preteen daughters. I'm sure you know where this story is going, but just in case you don't, the ranger recommended that the father take the very trail he tried to persuade us not to use! That ranger, for whatever reason, was and probably still is a BIPOC barrier.

BIPOC communities across America encounter this type of barrier daily. I want to be very clear that I do not believe that this type of barrier is a result of malice or detestation. It's not like that ranger woke up in the morning and said to himself, "What ruse shall I use to keep People of Color out of this park today?" Rather, he's simply a victim of his own unconscious bias. As numerous studies and research have determined, no human is exempt from unconscious bias and this ranger's bias is perfectly reinforced by the absence of People of Color, especially in ranger type jobs. Moreover, there is a very high probability that the ranger has led a racially segregated life.

Unconscious bias, lifelong racial segregation, and absence of People of Color all manifest themselves in acts of exclusion by outdoor gatekeepers like rangers. In addition, those being excluded, sustain these acts through passive act of acceptance. The ranger being exclusive, and the party being excluded was also culpable. Their culpability arises by allowing someone to direct them who only assumes their ability and level of experience, based on a narrow perspective and minimal experience working with their demographic. The cruelest act of outdoor exclusion is saying no to yourself and never showing up in the first place to be excluded.

In March of 2017, a group of OBA youth was recreating in theSan Gabriel Mountains National Monument outside of Los Angeles. They were playing in the snow, near a ski lift, when they were approached by an employee of one of the Forest Service vendors responsible for managing a nearby ski lift. This person asked the youth what they were doing there and proceeded to give them their marching orders by exclaiming, "Get the fuck out of here, this is Trump Country." The following week, the very same thing happened with another OBA group. This time the insult came from a different vendor employee. Our land management agencies have a public service duty to assure that the people they hire as vendors and concessionaires to work on our public lands will not harass, undermine, or otherwise deter underrepresented groups from showing up.

A few years back, a national park ranger in the Pacific Northwest got a frantic call from a camper who exclaimed that she and her husband needed an escort out of the campground. The ranger asked them why. She replied that she felt she was in danger. The ranger asked if a bear was in her campsite? She calmly replied, "No, it's a group of young people from the city." This woman was camping next to an OBA group who were all youth of color, and she was extremely uncomfortable and felt unsafe. The ranger inquired, "Is the group too loud or are they harassing you?" She answered no to both questions. So, the ranger asked her, "Then what is the problem?" She exclaimed, "We just don't feel safe!" The ranger did a wonderful job of solving the problem by asking her to leave the park and not to expect an escort.

For 64 years, OBA has been one of the oldest outdoor nonprofits in America dedicated to introducing urban and low-income groups of color to nature-based, conservation learning experiences. In years past, although not so much now, we used to joke about never having trouble getting a great campsite because as we move in, most White campers move out, as with the woman who requested the escort.

Diverse outdoor recreation is much more than promoting equitable access to the outdoors. It is about ending the ignorance that made that woman request an escort. It is about developing social responsibility, generating equity, and addressing the conspicuous absence of People of Color in the environmental and conservation professions. It is about espousing social reformation by promoting a more inclusive outdoor population that builds a community around stewardship of two of our most precious resources: people and the land.

Why diversify outdoor users? For over 40 years, I have been traveling this road and asking myself the same question. Now, I've come to the crossroads and can clearly see the answer. America's demographics are galloping into a burgeoning kaleidoscope of color at a remarkable clip. Our natural landscapes will be left in the dust of degradation if we do not engage, educate, and franchise the broader audience that will soon be responsible for protecting and conserving our natural landscapes.

The land is our unifying bond. It discriminates against only those who do not have access to it. It is the one thing that will carry us all into a common future. A statement that has been attributed to our Native American ancestors says it best: "We do not inherit the land from our ancestors; we borrow it from our children" (Unknown).

Lovingly submitted in honor of my dear friend Nina Roberts.

Photo courtesy of Outward Bound Adventures

The Woods

Kynetta Sugar McFarlane

Shaming is one of the deepest tools of imperialist, white supremacist, capitalist patriarchy because shame produces trauma and trauma often produces paralysis.

—bell hooks, Black feminist, activist, and writer

The Woods

I'm a trauma kid.

No, not just because I'm a Black,

queer,

half-immigrant, neurodivergent woman

that grew up in America.

My dad died when I was 7. I often felt different.

I couldn't express my feelings about how (weird, alone, scared, confused, angry, sad) I felt,

so I ate them.

I had a few activities that helped me express myself—reading and being in the woods.

Even though I was (AM)

a city girl,

I was lucky to have a backyard. A backyard with trees and birds and sunshine. I loved being in my backyard. With books,

I could go anywhere.

I was also a Girl Scout.

My Mom was a leader so I went on a lot of camp-ins.

I felt normal at Girl Scouts. I made so many friends there. I could express myself.

 I always knew I wanted to work with kids.

I also knew that I wanted to work with traumatized kids.

A lot of adults had been nice to me when I was struggling.

Who knew

I could combine my love of helping others, especially kids with the woods!!

I was able to watch kids

start to feel

normal and get their voice.

To remove

the shame of being (different,

poor, queer, abused, Hispanic, fat,

neurodivergent) themselves away.

References

hooks, b. (N.D.) bell hooks Quotes. Shame. https://www.azquotes.com/author/6871-Bell_Hooks/tag/shame

Without Gender

Lauren Mitten

When I was twelve, my mom came home one day after attending a meeting of the gay-straight alliance at the university where she taught and announced, "Lauren, I learned a new word today: genderqueer! I think I'm genderqueer!" She proceeded to explain the term: "genderqueer means not entirely a man and not entirely a woman."

I may have responded with something to the effect of "that's nice, mom," but hearing this did plant the seed of possibility in my head of being able to identify as something else. This is mystory of finding that something else, of concluding that I am agender, which is to say, without gender, and trying to tell you what that means to me.

There are many ways that my childhood was standard. We had a house and a dog. I went to public school and my parents separated when I was a kid. I fought with my parents and had fun times with them. But my parents were also lesbian feminists, and this added some unusual elements to my childhood.

My parents taught me to value women and to value being a woman. I was never told that "girls don't do that." It was clear to me that the fact that I was a woman didn't have to mean doing certain things and avoiding others.

But at fifteen and a sophomore in high school, when a university professor I was doing research with said to my mom, "she's such a smart and accomplished girl...er, young woman," I emphatically countered with, "person. Just person." I didn't want to hear that I was an accomplished young woman. I wanted to hear that I was an accomplished human, regardless of my gender. At the time, I was certain of this but not capable of articulating why.

Now I understand the reason I recoiled at the idea of my accomplishments being qualified with reference to a gender, specifically the "inferior" one. Plato wrote that "all the pursuits of men are the pursuits of women also, but in all of them a woman is inferior to a man" (Plato, 2019, p. 177). Being a woman today doesn't mean being considered inferior to the degree that it did in ancient Greece, but women are still judged to be lacking relative to men in many aspects of our culture. We all know what this looks like—unequal pay for equal work, a greater burden of housework, being used to sell products in sexist demeaning ways; the list goes on.

Although I grew up in a home where being a woman was a positive thing, I had begun to understand that outside that environment being a woman was not always seen as such. I didn't want to be a man, to be complicit in the patriarchy, enjoying male privilege at the expense of women, and still trapped by a different set of behavioral norms. But I didn't want everything that came with being a woman, either.

I fell in love with gender neutral pronouns after reading Marge Piercy's *Woman on the Edge of Time* as a first-year in college. I was thrilled by the way that the pronouns used in the utopian future Piercy described deemphasized gender, left it as a secondary characteristic, like hair color, rather than something immediately used to classify people as one thing or another, one better than the other. I loved this because it seemed to me to be a way of getting around the misogyny of our current society by deemphasizing gender, the ability of the patriarchal system to classify one half of people as less powerful would be hindered. Continuing in this line of thought, I also wondered if being genderqueer (the word I had at the time) could be a way of conveying personal feelings about gender and a revolutionary action, a refusal to stay within the system of gender that is used to oppress.

In college, I had classmates who came out as everything from genderfluid to third gender, and they asked people to use gender neutral pronouns for them. I had other classmates who came out as trans men or trans women and they asked people to change their pronouns accordingly. I knew I wanted to be androgynous, to look and act the way I was comfortable, with some feminine aspects and some masculine aspects, but it took time to figure out what this meant for me.

Here my early experiences around gender affected me in two rather contradictory ways. On the one hand, growing up less restricted by gender norms as many of my peers led me to more easily think about how my gender could be different than the one I was assigned at birth. On the other hand, my experiences led me to feel not only an attachment to the category of "woman" but also a solidarity with other women that I feared I would forsake if I stopped identifying as a woman.

Eventually, though, I decided that agender is the most accurate way to describe myself and is how I want people to understand me. I still have not resolved the question of whether I am letting "women" as a class down by linguistically, at least, renouncing my identity as a woman. But, for me, the degree of increased comfort I feel identifying as agender and my interest in modeling the freedom of living without gender won out, especially because not identifying as a woman does not mean that I will stop fighting gender-based oppression.

To me, being agender means rejecting the norms applied to any one gender and, at its core, rejecting the notion of gender entirely —just as atheists do not ascribe to some other religion orsome other god, but reject the notion of gods altogether, I reject the notion that a person has to have a gender, and I definitely reject the notion that I have to have a gender.

People I've come out to as agender in my personal life and at my generally liberal workplace are mostly very nice about it, and while many people struggle with using appropriate pronouns, they aren't being malicious. Even so, coming out is far from a one-time thing, and it has been hard for me to come out to everyone in my life— there are just so many people to come out to!

Imagine there's something core to your identity that you have to announce (and often explain) to nearly everyone you meet or risk them getting it wrong. For example, what if people constantly say things that assume you're Christian when being Jewish is an important part of your identity? I would imagine that even if you're terribly gregarious, it would be exhausting to have to "come out" to everyone you meet. And I dislike being the center of attention, particularly when I'm asking people to do something outside the norm and change the way they behave (e.g., using different pronouns for me).

But shy or not, I want to live in a world where people do not assume others' genders when they meet, just as people increasingly do not assume the gender of a new acquaintance's partner upon first mention. So, I will have those special conversations and try to push society towards that. I do this for myself, because it has been wonderful and freeing to have people understand me as agender and use gender neutral pronouns for me, and for the world, because the more people who are out and open about having nonnormative identities, the more the world will shift towards fewer assumptions and maybe even fewer restrictions based on gender—or perhaps the rejection of gender entirely.

When a somewhat old-fashioned executive used gender-neutral pronouns for me in an email, I got a heavy feeling in my heart. It was a feeling of great happiness and great sadness at once: happy that I—and people like me—are seen and validated by at least some small part of the world, and sad that so many more steps are needed to create the kind of world I truly want to live in, where people are free from the restrictions of gender. But I am appreciative that we might be moving in the right direction, and I'm ready to try to live in a way that is true to myself and work to speed us on that path.

References

Plato. (2019). *Republic*. (O. Markridis, Trans.). Chartwell Books. (Original work published ca. 380 B.C.E.).

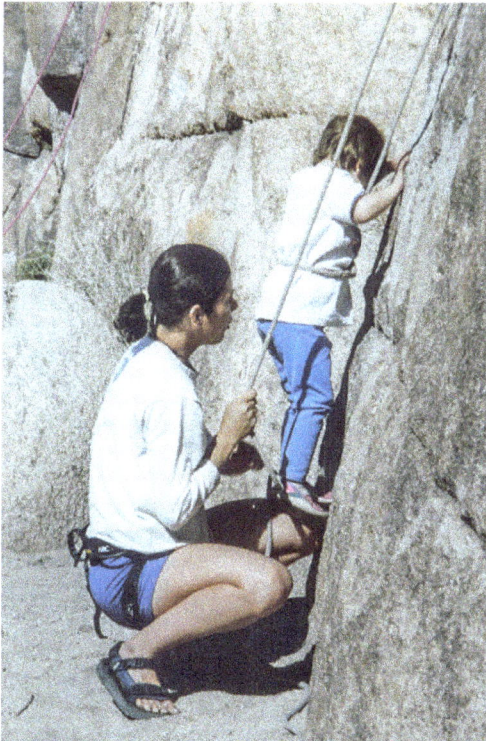

Photo courtesy of Denise Mitten

Building a Foundation of Trust

Bethany Facendini

While employed at a governmental organization serving a diverse population, I created an experiential education program called Teen Eco Action in cities that were known as the "toxic triangle" in the San Francisco Bay Area. The place-based program integrated environmental justice concepts, career exploration, multicultural environmental education, recreational activities, and stewardship projects by integrating themes that were relevant to young people's lives. Creating a sense of belonging for all in the outdoors was the overarching goal. Teen Eco Action aimed to remove actual and perceived barriers for participation to provide positive impactful connections with nature and each other. I needed to trust myself, my colleagues, the youth, their support networks, and the community to realize the intended program outcomes.

I was inspired to design a program for young people based on their expressed interests and needs after tenured colleagues at the governmental organization I worked for resisted changing an existing program with extensive resources to be more inclusive. Those colleagues valued tradition. If realizing equity meant modifying one of the agency's longest standing programs that catered to White, well-resourced families they were not open to change. These sentiments ignited me to increase meaningful community relationships and to develop a new program from the ground up. Although participants came from diverse backgrounds and had remarkable cultural wealth, Teen Eco Action was especially for youth of color and young people who lived in areas that were far from the basic resources they needed. Some of these included the lack of access to safe neighborhoods, high quality educational programs, healthy food, stable housing, adequate health care, clean air, and economic security, all shortcomings reflecting failed systems perpetuating racism. Teen Eco Action turned into an even greater opportunityto work with allies sharing the same devotion to social justice as me. This was an example of innovation happening at the grassroots level rather than the grasstops level.

In the early years of Teen Eco Action, I faced one of my most significant learning experiences as an outdoor educator. A parent did not want their son to participate in the program stating that he was not going to parks with a "do-gooder White lady." Despite my best efforts to assure her of her son's safety, staff qualifications, and overarching program benefits, she still said no. Deep listening and compassion were needed in this instance, not persuasive communication or a reaction from me about her comment. My heart was broken for the boy, who desperately wanted to attend, and for the pain and fear that generated this response from his mom's lived experience as a Black woman. I heard and understood her perspective, although it was different from mine. Several days later, she called me and said that he could come. I asked what changed her mind. She told me that his cousin, who previously had participated in the program, said that I live in the same community as they did, and that the program was great. I had earned enough trust for her to release some of her initial apprehensions. Establishing trust is paramount in any relationship, but especially for White people working in communities of color. It takes a demonstrated commitment for White people to educate themselves about racism and the systems that sustain it, show up with humility, value diverse experiences and perspectives, share resources, and follow the lead of People of Color as accomplices in racial justice work.

After participants completed Teen Eco Action, they received stipends. This was an aspect of removing barriers for their participation that was especially important for the youth of color and young people from low-income neighborhoods. The monetary award was usually distributed at a community celebration where other festivities highlighted the youths' accomplishments in the program. Kasi and his family did not attend, so I mailed his stipend to the address on his application. It was returned to me several weeks later. I reached out to him by phone offering to drop it off to him directly, and his mom gave me the address and a time to meet them. It's important to meet people where they are both literally and figuratively. When I arrived at the location, I immediately realized why he did not receive the correspondence. Kasi, his mother, and his two siblings and all their belongings lived in a sedan parked on a street in front of the address I was given on his application. His mother approached me first with a silent hug before I was greeted by the others. I gave Kasi his stipend, certificate, and Teen Eco Action photos. His mom said, "Kasi's dad will love to see these pictures of his son doing good. He has been in jail, and we are doing the best we can. It takes a village, Bethany, it takes a village." Hearing Kasi's happiness expressed about the program meant a lot to me during that moment, but I was struck by the transformation of his mother and my connection. For me, this will always remain as a powerful memory in experiential education.

I believe one of the most important tenets for advancing justice, equity, diversity, and inclusion is grounded in opportunities to see each other's humanity. Trusting each other and ourselves with open hearts is an aspect of this. Ultimately, this can encourage a sense of belonging and love that we all seek in ourlives. How will you be a part of the movement to actualize this?

Discussion Questions

Experiential learning is effective when it stimulates new ways of thinking, doing, and being with optimal engagement and reflection. These questions are for individual or group dialogue considering the context of your work to support advancing justice, equity, inclusion, and belonging. A safe space for all members needs to be ensured before addressing these topics in group settings.

♦   What are ways to build trust with individuals and communities?

♦   What is cultural wealth? What are examples of cultural wealth that you can identify in the communities you work with?

♦   What are some of the actual and perceived barriers to participation in your programs? What are innovative strategies that you can implement to overcome them?

♦   What levels of engagement do you have when designing and implementing programs for/with/by groups? How can you cocreate programs with the groups you want to serve or support them in creating their own programs?

♦   Have you experienced resistance to change when trying to make experiential education more diverse, equitable, and inclusive for all? If so, how did you address it?

♦   What is the White savior complex? Do you have examples of this from your experience?

♦   What are examples of systemic and institutional racism that surface in your organization and programs? How does White supremacy culture get perpetuated by you, your colleagues, and your organization? How and by whom is this being addressed?

Color the Parks Fantastic!

Aniko Kannas-Millan

I am proud to say that in 1994 I was the first Black woman Park Ranger hired at Santa Clara County Parks. I am disappointed to say I was still the only Black woman Park Ranger when I retired in 2020. In all that time, 26 years, only one other Black person, a man had been hired. How can that be in California? In the Bay Area?

In the last 10 years of my career, I appointed myself as a Ranger recruiter to help diversify our ranks. Successfully we hired and welcomed Asians, Latinos, queer, and more, but it was difficult as there was no pool of candidates to target easily. Department recruiting efforts were nonexistent unless my team and I created them while compromising an enormous workload and job priorities. The good news is at least I was not stopped from spending time on local recruiting, but it would have been great news to have been granted the necessary time and budget for further outreach.

As far as the shortage of black and brown faces in the queue, I feel it was because of the social injustices of the past and current barriers that have kept People of Color out of parks and nature. Many People of Color have hesitations about the "woods" as historically, our relatives were chased, hunted, and hanged there. It is a harsh but true reality that results in generation after generation cautioning and instilling fear rather than encouraging outdoor fun in nature. The same is seen in our visitation to the parks, with far fewer Black than White people enjoying park campgrounds and the trails. So how do we change this narrative and break down barriers so People of Color can happily benefit from all things beautiful outside in recreation and employment? On a greater necessary level, agencies must allow the dedicated time

55

and funding for concentrated outreach to attract more People of Color to both visit parks and apply for jobs. It is not enough to attend local career fairs or post fliers at Starbucks.

Time should be taken to build relationships with churches, colleges, and ethnic or cultural clubs and organizations such as university Black Student Unions and regional NAACP offices.

Additionally, mentor programs and internships should be established to prepare youth for careers in parks and the outdoors. An impressionable start to such efforts would be for the Junior Ranger program or ParkRx programs to target kids of color for a welcoming introduction with a friendly host. This is not difficult or costly, but it needs to be supported fully to work.

It is up to all of us, especially my BIPOC (Black, Indigenous, People of Color) brothers and sisters in the industry, to be a model for and mentor to our folks, so they realize the opportunities and feel safe outdoors. It was my modus operandi while on patrol to literally jump in front of Black visitors to the park to show them I was a Park Ranger and offer anything to make them feel welcomed and informed. With Black youth and young adults, I offered to share nature experiences and introduce them to outdoor fun. At the same time, I made it a point to teach about flora and fauna, to dispel myths, and to turn the "scary" into the "wow." I hope and expect others with this expertise to do the same. So here is the call to action, Parkies— Step It Up! Each one, teach one, reach one, and touch one.

Mainstreams and Margins

Margaret Lechner

At an Association for Experiential Education (AEE) conference in the late 70s, a group of organizational leaders participated in a sauna. Two of them reflected on the experience 40+ years later.

The Black man recalls, S. invited me to the sauna. I had never been in a sauna, but when in Rome do as the Romans do. I was a good swimmer (a lot of times there is a stereotype that Black guys can't swim), so Iput on my swimming trunks and headed down the moonlit path. I opened the door, and there ya'll were, some of you in your birthday suits. I was totally shocked. Someone invited me in, and the conversation began with the question about my program. Friendships developed.

The White woman recalls, we were walking down to the sauna and it occurred to me that this might be a very new experience for the one Black colleague in the group. I adjusted my walking pace to come alongside him and told him that the sauna was "clothing optional," and it's OK to wear clothes and it's OK to not wear clothes.

Two recollections on the same event. I (the White woman) now wonder how well we did at recognizing diversity, creating inclusion, and promoting equity?

♦ Inviting to the table. Yes.

♦ Recognizing differences in experience. A bit, although missing many levels.

- Sharing cultural knowledge and providing cues. Kind of. Creating focus on our shared purpose of learning about experiential programs. Yes.

Every group has a mainstream, where those people experience the comfort of knowing they belong. People in the mainstream habitually spend little energy thinking about group norms. People on the margin ask questions about belonging: "What can I do to fit in? Who are the gatekeepers who will help or hinder my movement toward the mainstream? Do I want to move toward the mainstream?" They are, as Sanford Tollette, Director of Pfeiffer Camp and the man in the scenario, described himself, "Calm on surface, but like a duck with feet paddling furiously; always observing and thinking." People can be in the mainstream in one situation (e.g., as camp director) and on the margin in another (first-time attender at an AEE conference). They shift along the continuum as they move from one interaction to another in a single setting. People who, on the surface, appear to be at one location on the mainstream-margincontinuum may be experiencing a different reality.

Looking further below the surface, the question "How well did we do at recognizing diversity, creating inclusion, and promoting equity?" has embedded mainstream assumptions. Being in the mainstream, the White speaker is confidently part of we. But who did we include? Was the Black colleague considered part of we? Why or why not? A statement of we can be a form of inclusion, but it also can have the subtext of "You are not part of we unless you do certain things or behave in certain ways." If they are going to be allies and help increase inclusion, people in the mainstream must behave like the duck paddling furiously, observing their own assumptions and actions, reflecting, and adjusting future actions.

We all can ask these questions:

- Where do I see examples of mainstreams and margins in other scenarios in this book and other places?

- What further insights can be gained from deeper reflection on this incident?

- What are the mainstream and margin dynamics in the groups I participate in regularly? In the groups I lead?

- If I am habitually in the mainstream, do I choose to put myself into situations where I am at the margins? What can I learn from this experience?

- When in the mainstream, am I attuned to the experiences of people at the margins? Do I check my assumptions and biases? How do I function as a gatekeeper?

References

Hunter, D. (2022). Training for Change. https://www.trainingforchange.org/training_tools/mainstream-margin/

Photo courtesy of Brad Faircloth

Reflections on My Experience Developing the First Indigenous Youth Program to be Recognized as Evidence-based

McClellan (Mac) Hall

My name is McClellan (Mac) Hall (Cherokee), and I am the founder of the National Indian Youth Leadership Project (NIYLP), the developer of Project Venture, as well as a former Association for Experiential Education (AEE) Board member, Kurt Hahn recipient, and one of the founders of the Natives, Africans, Asians, Latino(a)s, and Allies (NAALA) group. NIYLP is a New Mexico-based nonprofit with a 35-year track record. NIYLP developed the Project Venture model, which now has served over 100 communities. The inspiration for Project Venture came to me in a dream in the late 1970s. I didn't understand the meaning and filed it away for later. Several years later, I met Crosslin Smithe, an elder, traditional medicine man, and spiritual leader at the Cherokee Nation in Vian, Oklahoma. He became my mentor, interpreted my dream, and explained to me, "This is what you've been asked to do, through this dream." He added that I was to create programming for Indian youth that had Indigenous culture as its foundation. With his support, I created Project Venture, an Indian youth program modeled on our Indigenous culture.

In 1990, NIYLP received a 5-year High Risk Youth Demonstration Grant from Substance Abuse and Mental HealthServices (SAMHSA). The program focused on four Indigenous communities in New Mexico. Our evaluation data were outstanding. We measured substance abuse prevention outcomes through an indirect Positive Youth Development approach, using outdoor adventure, service learning, and Indigenous culture (Carter et al., 2007; Springer et al., 2004). Our data from this 5-year project drew the attention of the federal agency (SAMHSA) sponsor of the National High RiskYouth Study.

Project Venture was funded for a 3-year follow-up grant from SAMHSA and expanded to new communities. Project Venture was found to be the most effective program for American Indian and Alaska Native Youth in the National High Risk Youth Study (2002). Our data and results were stronger than many of the non-Indigenous programs studied. The director of the study, Dr. Fred Springer, wrote a letter to NIYLP, acknowledging our outstanding results. In addition, Dr. Springer found that Project Venture contained all eight of the characteristics of the most effective programs found in the study.

Based on these data, results, and consistent evaluation outcomes, Project Venture received the Promising, Effective andModel Program awards in consecutive years. We were the first Indigenous-developed program to achieve evidence-based status. However, in the process of being reviewed by a distinguished panel of social scientists and academic researchers for the Model Program Award, our data were reviewed three times. This seemed unusual. We believe that thereviewers didn't think that an Indigenous program could achieve such positive results. Yet our evaluator, Dr. Susan Carter, one of the top evaluators in the field, continued to advocate for our program.

After nearly a year, we finally received the Model Program Award. This is one of numerous awards and recognitions we have received over 30 years, including the Milestone Program award from the Kellogg Foundation, Exemplary Program Awards from First Nations Behavioral Health Association, Spirit of Crazy Horse Award, Alec Dickson Servant Leadership Award, Indian Health Service Behavioral Health Award, and many more.

In our work with youth, we understand that we need to work in both the seen and unseen worlds. Reconnecting young people with the natural world is critical. Engaging elders has been an important part of our work. Dr. Jane Goodall is a friend and partner in our work. It was important to stay true to the vision and not allow our program to be influenced or intimidated by academics or funders who didn't see the potential of what we were doing.

We have tried to stay true to Indigenous values and respect traditional knowledge. It's never been about money or recognition, just developing a generation of resilient Indigenous youth. Although much of our original funding was for substance abuse prevention, our approach is indirect, based on positive youth development, social emotional learning, and cultural approaches and focused on developing resilient young people. We have encountered bias in several areas, including from funders, yet we have remained true to the dream and the advice from elders who have guided our work. We have a diverse board of Indigenous people from the United States, including Hawaii, and Canada, as well as non-Indigenous professionals who believe in our work.

I think our presence as an Indigenous outdoor adventure program within the AEE (beginning in the 1980s) has inspired People of Color to come to AEE and feel comfortable. We still have a way to go in terms of diversity, but we have opened doors and hopefully helped others to feel welcome.

References

Springer, J. F., Sale, E., Hermann, J., Sambrano, S., Kasim, R., & Nistler, M. (2004). Characteristics of effective substance abuse prevention programs for high-risk youth. *Journal of Primary Prevention, 25*(2), 171–194.

Carter, S. L., Straits, J. E., & Hall, M. (2007). Project Venture: Evaluation of a positive, culture-based approach to substance abuse prevention with American Indian youth. Technical Report. The National Indian Youth Leadership Project. Gallup, NM. www.niylp.org

Photo courtesy National Indian Youth Leadership Project

Reflections on the Glass Ceiling: Then and Now

Sky Gray

I was in college in 1983 taking an outdoor adventure pursuits class when my professor referenced Marilyn Loden (1987), who used the term "glass ceiling" in 1978. My professor invited discussion as to why women were to blame for the barriers preventing women from advancing their careers in a male-dominated world. Dr. Wise also spoke of the deeper issues that historically kept women from occupying positions of authority, the glass ceiling being the primary cause. She was trying to prepare us for things to come. While I was no stranger to gender and racial inequalities that existed at that time, I felt compelled to more fully understand the dominant Euro-American systems that constructed these barriers. That was the beginning of a long and, at times, painful quest. I share this personal journey to support women who are walking their own path towards equality as they break their own glass ceilings (we still only make 83 cents to every man's dollar) and to hopefully raise awareness and consciousness for men as well.

Fortunately, I had strong women role models, and thankfully, my mom was one of them. She was a businesswoman and entrepreneur and urged me to never give up or let my dreams be daunted by the glass ceiling or anything else. I took her advice to heart, and I listened to her words, along with trusted others, and acted accordingly. I knew then, like I know now, as a woman, I would have to work harder, pay my dues, prove my worth, suck it up, withstand many of our societal isms, and achieve an advanced degree to advance into leadership positions. With steely determination, I was ready to take on the world to break barriers, to call out injustice, and to break glass ceilings. Like many women, I had no idea just how hard that would be and how challenging it would be to gain a seat at the table.

In 1984, I attended my first Association for Experiential Education (AEE) conference with Virginia Commonwealth University's Outdoor Adventure Club at Lake Junaluska, North Carolina. It paved the way for a 40-year trajectory of doing my best trying to make the world a better place through experiential education. At this conference, I found my calling, my cause, and my people. I noted signs posted about women getting together to share stories and support. I remember thinking how cool that was. However, I never went to the women's meeting at the first conference or the second, as I was too afraid to be seen or stereotyped as a separatist, radical feminist, or lesbian. These were labels used by the dominant heteropatriarchy to keep women in their place. These fears did not come out of the blue; there were many critical judgments made and questions asked, mostly by men, about why women and eventually People of Color needed their own safe spaces and affinity groups. The realization of the importance of having affinity spaces for marginalized AEE members stuck with me. These early experiences and conferences also enabled me to recognize my deep internalized oppression and the need to unpack my White privilege as well. The glass ceiling and "isms" were becoming more real as I encountered different scenarios.

Fast Forward...

Well into early 1993, I knew I had to continue my education, as the glass ceiling was ever present and so was my desire to contribute more. After my many formative years at the Santa Fe Mountain Center (SFMC), I got a teaching assistantship and an eventual master's degree at Aurora University. I studied under Dr. Rita Yerkes, one of AEE's trailblazers in social justice work. Her unrelenting support of women in the outdoors inspired me, and so many others, beyond measure.

Before heading off to get my master's degree, I was logging 140+ days per year in the field leading wilderness programs, ropes courses, river trips, and camps at the SFMC. Those were amazing times of doing mission driven, heartfelt work with some of the most marginalized youth and adults in New Mexico. However, I knew it was time to advance my knowledge, stretch my comfort zones and hone more skills. I also knew to advance my career, I had to further my education. I was supported and encouraged to take on leadership roles within AEE, thus acting upon my dreams to advance social justice and equity work. My consulting business (Challenge to Change) kept me afloat until my credentials, experience, and hard work landed my dream job as Director of Accreditation for AEE. As the first woman to serve in this role, another glass ceiling was broken.

It was an exciting time for AEE and for the advancement of risk management standards in the experiential adventure education field. I was privileged to work side by side with Betty van der Smissen, Jeff Little, Mike Gass, Bill Zimmerman, Rita Yerkes, Deb Ajango, Steve Pace, Reb Gregg, Jane Panicucci, Jed Williamson, Dick Prouty, Molly Hampton, Jude Hirsch, and others. We worked to ensure that the accreditation program was advocated for and institutionalized as a core driver of excellence within AEE. Those years working with such a dynamic group of dedicated volunteer leaders were some of the best times in my professional career. There was a lot of teamwork, mutuality, equity, and shared respect on the council. It felt so empowering. Other women and I felt seen, respected, and valued by this passionate group, as we worked tirelessly to advance the accreditation program. However, when Arthur Conquest and others challenged the AEE board and Executive Director about the lack of People of Color, representation, and inclusivity within the membership, I knew the leadership of AEE and I needed to do more.

That's when my soul sister, Dr. Nina Roberts, an AEE board member at the time, and I joined forces. We both noted that the outdoor adventure field at large and the AEE accreditation standards needed more cultural inclusion, humility, and competence. In 2000, we merged our respective consulting companies and were fired up to spread the word. We conducted numerous trainings and workshops for the Wilderness Risk Management Conference and AEE. We consulted with organizations and published a variety of articles in journals and proceedings on culture, competency, and risk. We cocreated the first humanist risk management model (Gray & Roberts, 2004), which was hailed at the time as trailblazing. A variety of these concepts were then incorporated into the AEE accreditation standards, and many programs used our model as a programmatic tool.

About that time, the Santa Fe Mountain Center (SFMC) beckoned again. SFMC was experiencing deficits and a crisis of confidence on whether it should continue as a 501(C3). I was offered the executive director position and I accepted.

The SFMC board gave me a directive to either shut the organization down or build it back up. I choose the latter. The fiscal and programmatic challenges came with vast opportunities to create an inclusive, diverse vision, mission, and set of values that put the historically well-known SFMC back on the map. I brought in Nina to conduct diversity trainings and she rocked the house (the converted chicken coop headquarters of the SFMC). A great team was built with the right people, and the SFMC grew by leaps and bounds programmatically and fiscally, with many strong, diverse women leaders throughout the organization. A renewed recognition for SFMC, locally and nationally, was gained.

Coupled with the successes, the next 16 years were a combination of breaking barriers, addressing gender bias, homophobia, and sexism at the board and staff level, and working on my cultural humility and competence as well as managing a variety of organizational challenges that came with our expanded mission, fundraising, and diverse programming. As the longest serving Executive Director, second was my friend and mentor Dr. Rocky Kimball, who founded the SFMC in 1979, the time came for me to pass the baton and metaphorically the "rope." Nina had been a catalyst for change and recruited me to direct the Pacific Leadership Institute at San Francisco State University. In addition to that prospect, I had been presented with another amazing career opportunity in Northern California (Sonoma County), and I knew the time was right to cook up more change and deepen my work in leading trauma-informed care transformation. It was an offer I could not refuse and that has netted much personal and professional growth. Rocky came to Santa Fe to celebrate my retirement from SFMC and to support our leadership transition by reminding us of our roots and history.He provided me with wise counsel and a book about life's reimagined moments. I was so grateful for both, as Rocky had a big influence on me and believed in me as a young experiential educator and therapeutic wilderness instructor. He saw something in me back then and supported my aspirations at SFMC and beyond. It paid off and I am grateful for him to this day.

Like most women moving through their careers, I incurred moments and incidents of bumping into the glass ceiling, gender bias, gaslighting, and overt and covert sexism. I also incurred moments of clear support, care, and allyship. If women choose to advance their careers and step into leadership positions, they most often have to confront the ceiling and related gender dynamics on many occasions. In my current role as a program manager for Sonoma County Human Services at Valley of the Moon Children's Center, I am fully supported by an all-woman leadership team and a diverse management team. My former division director, an amazing man and role model, is one of the most culturally humble directors I have served under. He is a true ally. He walks his talk, and I will forever be grateful for him, as he has led us through some challenging times such as fires and floods and helped lead diversity, equity, inclusion, and belonging (DEIB) efforts, including a new antiracist and DEIB vision and mission.

The work we are doing as an agency to become an antiracist, inclusive, trauma-informed, and more diverse organization is compelling, messy, and, at times, exacting. To this end, our new Division Director, who is an amazing trauma-informed woman, and the entire human services division are promoting and leading us in training in deep DEIB work with a trauma-informed care lens. This gives me hope as we seek to right the wrongs of the isms and barriers that so many marginalized people still face. I share parts of my journey to illustrate the barriers and highlight the collective boldness it takes all of us to transcend them. So, if you find yourself bumping or crashing into the glass ceiling, gender bias, or being set up on the glass cliff, take heed, don't back down, find your people, buckle up, and don't give up. Remember… as Ruth Bader Ginsberg reminds us, "well behaved women rarely make history." Make your voice heard.

In closing, Nina and I often talked about the call to action when her fight for social justice became disheartening and exhausting as she faced her own glass ceilings, gender-biased dynamics, and racism. We vowed never to give up or turn a blind eye on our shared passions around promoting social justice. We also talked about how important men allies are in supporting us in the quest for justice. We appreciate you and we need you, too! It is essential for organizations to reckon with present day glassceilings, racism, sexism, homophobia, historical transgressions, "isms," and White supremacy culture. I was blessed to find a friend, mentor, and social justice warrior like Nina. Collectively, as professions using experiential education methodology, let's remember that we are not alone in the struggle for DEIB. We stand on the shoulders of giants who have helped pave the way for a more just and compassionate world. Nina was a giant for me and for many. May we all rise up and carry her social justice torch forward.

Recommendations

- Identify allies that help you grow and deepen your understanding of DEIB.

- Personally identify with issues of DEIB.

- Find women or allied men who help you navigate breaking the glass ceiling or other barriers and gender dynamics.

- Find ways to do DEIB in your work and personal life and seek the support you need to do so.

References

Loden, M. (1987). Recognizing women's potential: No longer business as usual. *Management Review*, *76*(12), 44.

Gray, M.S. & Roberts, N.S. (2004). Culture, competency, and risk: The mystery and crossroads continue. In C. Jones (Ed.), Proceedings of the 2004 Wilderness Risk Management Conference, (pp. 27–31) NOLS.

Photo courtesy of Sky Gray

Resiliency Rising

D. Maurie Lung

As early as I can remember, I have wanted to work in the field of outdoor education. In fact, after a particularly impactful summer resident camp experience, I wrote, in my well-worn second-grade Strawberry Shortcake diary, "When I grow up, I want to help people in the out-of-doors."

I think part of what made that camp experience so impactful is that I felt included, wanted, and protected from the world around me. So, I followed this path in both my education and occupation as a camp counselor, ropes course director, nature center specialist, camp director, adventure therapist, and finally as the CEO of a nonprofit community-based counseling center that provides nature-based and adventure-based counseling.

As ideal as my growing up experiences were, I was not prepared for my first "real" job after college graduation as an outdoor program specialist in Alabama. At 23 years old, I was hired to create programs that help youth connect to the natural world and to the people around them. It seemed ideal. Within a few months, I had full programs and lots of excitement for potential opportunities.

Growing up in the South and other more conservative areas, I was not naïve about the potential social justice and human rights issues. I had been yelled at and attacked at my own apartment building while I was taking out the garbage to the apartment community dumpster. Nevertheless, I was shocked when my CEO pulled me aside during the planning and preparation months for summer camp and stated, "I know you are hiring a lot of summer staff right now. If you suspect any of them are gay, fire them for any reason you can. We don't want those people to influence our

71

youth." Those people. It was then I clearly understood that I was "those people." I quickly turned to, how am I supposed to fire myself? Or do I out myself and get fired? Or do I quietly resign? I never thought of talking with human resources, because, at that time, it was perfectly legal to fire someone for being gay. And frankly, it still happens. All. Of. The. Time.

I was young. I had few, if any, resources yet. I had no representation in my field that I knew of yet. I had no allies that I was aware of yet. So, I resigned on a Friday, cancelled my apartment lease on Saturday, rented a U-Haul and drove to California without a job, and without knowing anyone there, on Sunday.

Over time, I have learned resilience. I have learned how to find my allies. I have learned how to be visible so that others are not so alone. Navigating this process was overwhelming at times. Mostly, I just dove in and tried to learn and familiarize myself with LGBTQIA+ social justice issues and what is being done about them. History helped me create a foundation of my path forward.

In California, I found several community organizations where I could connect with other similarly-minded folks as well as find a place where I didn't have to worry so much about how I was showing up and if my being alive would offend someone. I got more involved with voting, talking with representatives, and following legislation that impacts the LGBTQIA+ community. I attended protests and demonstrations and my first Pride Parade. I spoke out. Again and again. Through social media, presentations, and with friends.

Thirty years later, these still feel like trying times. Now, as aparent, I have the duty to help navigate my children through these situations and create space for dialogue, healing, and action. Sometimes, I forget that there are allies or people who want to create compassionate change in our world. Connecting with allies and being open with our stories and with the questions that sometimes follow helps me engage allies in more effective interventions.

Being targeted daily—at the grocery store, when I take my children to the playground, at the PTA meeting—is stressful and exhausting. And yet, whenever I start to feel hopeless about the people around me, I am reminded by my children or a colleague about how important our work of experiential education is today. To bring these social injustices to the attention of our society, experiential educators create experiences for people to connect with each other as well as to the world around them in a most human way. We can heal some of the cracked hearts in our world by creating corrective experiences. It doesn't erase what happened. It can mitigate what happened. It may create opportunities to build resiliency skills. Teaching and practicing care, such as tending to a plant or practicing Leave No Trace practices, helps us with the skills of caring for others and skills of resiliency.

Finally, I continue to search for common ground with others around me, and with compassion, while still being authentic and visible. My children remind me that we teach others to be kind by being kind to others. They remind me that we all have our stories and unique circumstances of our life. They remind me to create space to deeply listen to other's truths. These spaces, where people can be witnessed and heard, help with healing and restoration of dignity.

Be the Change: Speaking Up, Stepping in It (Sometimes), and Being an Ally

Chris Heeter

There's a fine line between leaning into your true wild nature—who you are at your core, nothing to fix or improve, just you in all your beauty, messiness, naturalness, and quirkiness—and identifying things you can address or overcome that do not compromise your true self. For me, my near debilitating desire not to upset people isn't really a wild characteristic; it's just a comfortable default. I'm overall likeable, but I'm not even sure my desire not to upset people particularly enhances this quality, as if that were a higher mark than real and honest discourse. I'm inspired by people who dare to step out of their comfort zone. And I'm especially moved when someone demonstrates awareness of the struggles that others face and risks "stepping in it" or "saying it wrong" to speak up about an injustice they witness or to promote equality or equity.

It is really powerful to be on the receiving end of this type of allyship. I remember such a moment during one of my week-long Wilderness First Responder certification courses. Frankly, the instructors were being jerks, calling the women (those who appeared feminine) "doll" and "girls" while calling the men (those who appeared masculine) "bro" and "dude." They were consistently sexist, and the group members could tell the instructors were unaware (or didn't care) that their language was creating a negative learning environment.

In our final training scenario, which is always a long, crazy wilderness disaster where the instructors throw in all kinds of kinks along the way, we chose a woman as our incident commander. The instructors role-played as helicopter pilots who flew in to take away the most severely injured people. They were complete and total jerks to our incident commander, who handled them with confidence and clarity.

In our debrief, as people tried to discuss the instructors' treatment of the commander, they insisted that this is what it is like out there and how women will be treated. One young man in our group spoke up and said that it seemed likely the women in the course were deeply familiar with that kind of behavior and probably have a long list of methods for dealing with it. The young man suggested to the instructors that they could "be the change" and offer constructive ideas on ways to handle tense situations rather than reinforce old stereotypes. It was so powerful that a young, White man said this. For sure, it took courage to speak like that to these guys. And as a benefactor of his words, it just felt so good to not have to go through the machinations of whether to say anything—what people would think, whether anyone would back me up, and if saying anything would risk my certification that had to be submitted by these instructors.

I appreciated this young man's comments because far too often people from majority groups aren't paying attention. Consciously or otherwise, many people preserve the status quo, believing that it favors them, instead of using their power to effect change.

Right now, there is an aching need for more people to pay better attention to how women, People of Color, and all who are perceived as having different experiences, are treated during meetings and other gatherings. It's a call to stay alert to inequities and disparities and to bring our wild nature forward, daring to notice and speak up.

Being a leader calls for awareness and self-reflection, attending to how we are perceived and received as leaders, particularly when we're trying to demonstrate our expertise. As vulnerability and courage expert Brene Brown (2021) says, having to be the "knower" or always being right—as my instructors were—is heavy armor. It's defensiveness, it's posturing, and, worst of all, it leaves no room for connection, other perspectives, and more informed decisions.

It's also very common because our dominant culture reinforces and rewards knowing, being right, and not asking for help. Unfortunately, needing to know everything is pretty miserable for the knowers and everyone around them. It leads to distrust, bad decisions, and unnecessary and unproductive conflict.

For me, I know that I can take on more risk in terms of noticing and speaking up in the face of stereotypes and insulting language and behavior. It means I'll step in it sometimes, but that's really not the end of the world. I can regroup, learn, apologize, and hopefully get it right next time. I sure appreciated the young man suggesting that the instructors "be the change." Even if he said something less eloquent, I would have appreciated his effort. There would have been room for dialogue between us, an opportunity for further understanding.

While not comfortable, especially for this introvert, it seems a fair trade to speak up so that the people directly experiencing whatever the tired old comments and assumptions are don't have to always decide whether to advocate for themselves. At this time, when our country is so locked into our various beliefs, I am inspired by that ally of mine.

I invite you to join me in a wild dare I am setting for myself: I want to be the change, to speak up more, and be a more present and supportive ally. I want to encourage, nudge, and support leaders to be open and curious about ways to shift, as Brene Brown (2021) says, from wanting to "be right" to wanting to "get it right."

References

Brown, B. (2021, March 22). Hello Monday. LinkedIn. https://
     www.linkedin.com/pulse/bren%C3%A9-brown-getting-right-its-fear-
     gets-way-daring-armor-jessi-hempel/

Photo courtesy of the Roberts Family

The Other Side of the Mountain

TA Loeffler

My outdoor and experiential education career has been draped in the cloak of "not being enough." In many settings, in the eyes of the instructors who trained me and the view of my co-instructors who I worked with, I have never been tall enough, fastenough, strong enough, technically skilled enough, and, as so often is the case, it didn't take much for that cloak to slip from them to me to occlude my perception of self, body, and skills. I remember, in an early career climbing course, being almost dragged uphill on a rope team at a pace I couldn't sustain. My glacier glasses were fogging. I was getting sweaty, and the instructor yelled expletives at me for taking my glasses down trying to get them to clear. He offered no relief from the pace nor instruction on how to keep them from fogging. I internalized this as one of my first outdoor experiences of being "not fast enough."

In a high-angle rescue course, the male students tended to grasp the technical systems faster than the women on the course. They would very quickly take the ropes and carabiners out of the women's hands to speed up the process of setting up the systems during scenarios. To prevent this from happening to me, I spent hours hauling chairs around the kitchen with mini versions of the systems every evening. There was inadequate practice time before the members were placed into higher stakes scenarios where the students naturally gravitated to gender-based roles— the men did most of the technical tasks while women did support in the back, away from the cliff's edge. The instructor did not assist the group members in shifting this division of tasks, even though it is critical that each learner gets ample practice in all tasks and roles. This was another moment when women were seen as "not fast enough," and our learning suffered from that inaccurate perception.

Similarly, I have had expedition leaders comment about my appearance, my speed, and my abilities in hurtful ways. One expedition leader kept a publicly-posted whiteboard of travel times through the Khumbu icefall with a "line of shame" drawn across an arbitrary line demarking the edge between the pace that was fine and the pace that was too slow. There were many more women below the line than above. This public shaming cemented the internalization that I could never be "fast enough," impacting my ability to truly assess whether my pace was adequate to ensure my safety.

On a subsequent climb, we were given reference times for our moves between camps. Although I was solidly in the middle (i.e., my move to advanced base camp was 3.6 hours while the range given was 2–6 hours), I labelled myself as "slow." I squirm now as I type this because I recognize that I was stuck in a mind trap of shaping my experience by internalizing that I was slow and therefore inadequate. The irony is that, on that day, it really didn't matter how long it took to go from basecamp to advanced base camp because there were absolutely no hazards requiring speed to minimize exposure to danger. All the above experiences mix in my thoughts to make both my backpack and mind heavier—I'm distracted by the constant discourse of "not being OK and not belonging" while outdoors.

My sense of humor is always at the ready to help me cope when facing adversity or oppression. I often channel my inner stand-up comedian when the going gets rough to assist myself and others in having the support of a joyful mind. I also dig in, work hard, and remind myself that this moment will change and shift, essentially creating space so that I can see a path to change up the dynamic or set a course for a more just outcome.

Amid the kinds of moments mentioned above, I am helped by others' belief in me. When I cannot see my competency or "fineness," supportive mentors, peers, and friends remind me that, whether I can see it in a particular moment, I am ok and enough despite dominant messaging in the world and outdoor education in specific. They have, through notes they sent with me into the field or through reflection dialogue after an expedition, assisted me in countering the dominant narrative of being lacking. Much like the sun that is still up there on cloudy days even if we can't see it, having supportive folks hold up my basic goodness when I could not was critical to me staying in the field, gaining skills, and eventually finding a path to where I could see it most days.

On occasion, allies intervened and interrupted such interactions through both direct and indirect actions such as holding space, asking for changes in instructional style, slowing down to match pace, listening, coaching, creating additional practice sessions, and the like. Other allies have created gender-inclusive training materials, practices, and research to move our fields away from these inaccurate and harmful beliefs and teaching methods.

I call for all who use experiential education in their fields to critically examine the foundational beliefs that our practices have been built on. This can help root out more of the ingrained ways that various oppressions still flourish and indeed may still be propagated. Although so many have advocated for change for so long, some programs still leave others behind and fail to be accessible to all. Leaders encourage glorifying one group over another. Seeking ways to ensure that everyone can climb their figurative or literal mountains in whatever way makes sense for them and that when people reach their various summits, everyone feels welcomed and valued there.

Rock Climbing and Diversity, Equity, Inclusion, and Belonging Lessons

Amelia Tarren

I've always wanted to climb Maniac. Maniac is a Rosetta Stone of glassy grey granite rising out of the sea along the Maine coast. Its difficulty is 5.14 on a scale of 5.0–5.15, ranging from stepping up mountainous rocks to climbing up nearly blank walls, often steep with few holds. I feel most at home in this place. Therefore, I travel there as often as I can because everyone deserves to go where they feel most alive.

I've been back three times to attempt Maniac. I have not completed, or sent it, not even close. Each visit has been marked by different lessons and stages in my own identity development. To understand my connection to my identity as an Asian woman in the outdoors, I share lessons I have learned each time I returned from attempting to climb Maniac in Maine.

First Lesson: Nature and Identity

It is important to be proud of my strengths. As an adopted Chinese woman, I have the strong, thin, and elegant body of a goddess for rock climbing.

I find solace in the outdoors because it helps to feel less alone—when I cannot find a peaceful sense of self, I can still find a sense of place. The beauty of nature is just so vast it's hard to think about anything else.

Everywhere I go, I carry a little bit of worry, a certain alertness, minuscule moments of overcoming a thought about a quiet racist comment or wondering if looking like a coronavirus spreader warranted the lack of a gracious smile from a stranger. In nature, I don't think about microaggressions because I am so present in the moment.

I've always felt alive at the ocean; however, my love for the coast deepened when I found rock climbing. I learned the noise of doubt could be quelled the minute I pulled on the wall—the silence, the focus, dialing in, edging upward. Elegance resolving the need for strength. The belief that says you don't need to be a muscle-man. You need to be you—agile, strong, clever. Just this part of a woman, this woman, works well right here.

The area around Maniac, Quoddy Head, has always been important to me. I love how whales are constantly rising up around the bay, gasping big sonorous breaths of sea spray. I love the long sunsets framed by the silhouettes of fir trees. I love the feel of the rockweed and the sound of the tide straining up and down the coastline. At the ocean cliff, I'm whole—the expanse is so vast, space to hold all the heartache in the world.

For me, these experiences and sensations are not identity based; rather, the sensations of nature are universal despite the messages that nature should be off limits for some people. The coastline of Maine represents home, family, expanse, and goodness. I am free to not worry here.

Second Lesson: Women and Climbing

It is difficult to remain on the climbing scene without the validation of a White man.

From my experience, the acceptance of a diverse individual in heteronormative White spaces depends on the validation by those in the dominant culture. Historically, climbing has been the domain of White men; however, in the past decade, it has shifted to more diverse populations with the emergence of a more gymnastic emphasis in climbing. Gymnastics is suited to the smaller, more flexible bodies of women. However, to be accepted, women and BIPOC people must gain favor from the dominant gatekeepers.

The social barrier of entry into climbing is high for women. I think the challenge of receiving unwanted advice, or mansplaining, and the idea of wilderness being unsafe for women causes many women to feel uncomfortable going out in their own groups.

A heteronormative phenomenon also plays out on the cliff. I notice that women express their frustration through tears rather than the secondary anger men are permitted to show. However, supported by a boyfriend, a woman crying honestly while failing seems less obtrusive to the rest of the climbers present because the man is protecting the woman. In contrast, two women climbing partners expressing vulnerability is viewed as an obtrusive weakness.

I think the notion of needing to be a superhero for women in climbing is also unfair. Women climbers are expected to be exemplary to be respected by male climbers. The constant pressure to be a superwoman or be annexed out of the climbing community weighs on me.

I challenge the definition of "being enough" compared to someone else. Success is not about being "woman" or "man" enough or even ascending the climb. Enough should be defined by being present and enjoying the process of overcoming personal barriers along the way. However, holding onto this is so difficult. The validation of a woman by a man is necessary to blend in with the bro-pack of climbing. However, it's a Catch-22 as being validated or protected by a man doesn't let women be respected for their own merits.

Mainstream rock-climbing media is based on the notion that men are stronger and therefore better climbers. Additionally, much of climbing is continuing to get back on the wall and failing repeatedly. Therefore, climbing success is defined by completing the rock climb and, in the process, managing repetitive failure along the way.

For me, it's complicated. I live with the belief that I was not kept by my birth parents because I would not be as strong as a man, who would be more useful in the Chinese rural countryside. I think proving that I am physically capable in the sport lends itself to overcoming this stereotype when I am successful, and, on the downside, feeling immense failure when I am unable to complete a rock climb. I do like how understanding geometry or body position helps me excel at climbing. This is a reparative experience because it assures me the stereotype of women not being strong enough is challenged by a woman's ability to be clever and creative in solving the climb. After years of being told I should be good at geometry and math because I'm Asian, I decided I might as well use my understanding of geometry, which is one of the most important skills in being a strategic and smart climber, even more important than raw strength.

I contended with these social barriers by trying to go after Maniac, one of the most elite climbs in the Northeast. Was I validated, was I enough, did I need to be a superwoman, could I show my feelings? Climbing for a BIPOC woman is so much more than clipping the anchors.

Third Lesson: Collective Belonging

There is no better way to quell the frustration of an unfair world than to let climbing be an equalizer between diverse people.

People often perceive mountaineering and climbing as solo activities, as if climbers summit alone. In this third lesson, I challenge the idea of climbing alone, since so many people build the pathway to success and deserve the shared credit.

To address DEIB at the cliff, the climbing community can't go it alone. Current climbing organizations will need to reexamine their missions to embrace social justice. For example, they can refine the notion of access beyond building parking lots, conserving land, and doing trail work. Access should also include ways for diverse populations to have equitable climbing experiences. This requires allocating funding for DEI trainings and initiatives, ensuring that boards of directors and other stakeholders are representative of oppressed groups, and searching for and listening to silenced voices. I also believe that creating affinity groups such as Outdoor Asians, a group dedicated to building a diverse and inclusive community of Asian and Pacific Islanders in the outdoors, hold new potentials for collective success.

Maniac has given me a sense of place and of purpose. I hope aspiring women and BIPOC climbers one day visit this place with a desire to climb and a sense of collective belonging.

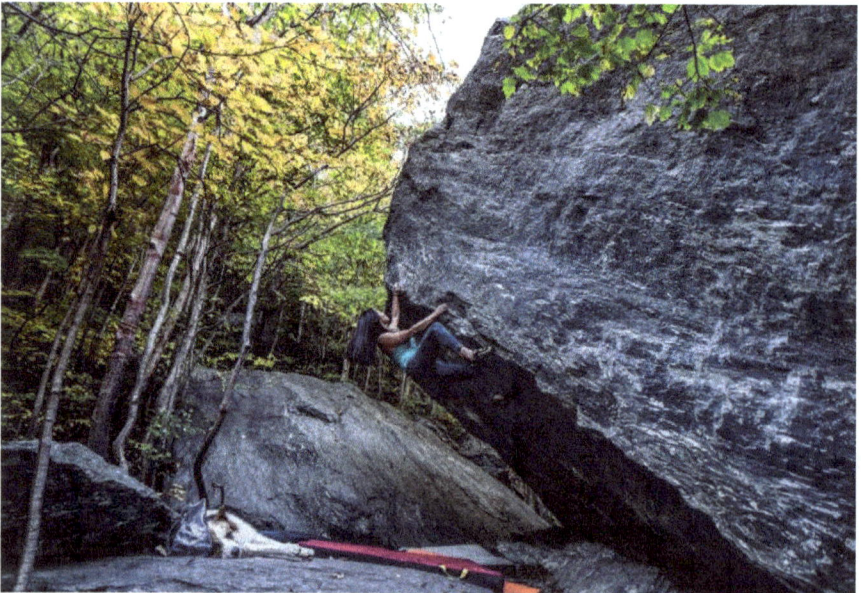

Photo courtesy of Tim Kemple

Bold Not Bossy: Asking Girls to Lead in Outdoor Spaces (and Beyond)

Priscilla McKenney

I wanted to get up among the clouds and to feel myself free as the birds and the air and to be able to shout my freedom as loudly as I liked, and not have someone point and sadly say, 'it is not pretty for little girls to climb'.

—Alma Wagen (1923)—the first women guide on Mt. Rainier in Washington, United States.

I just awoke from a night of sleeping on this granite ledge under the stars. I sit in the quiet and stillness of the morning overlooking an alpine meadow at 274 meters (9000 feet). Singing birds are the only sounds that break the silence. The strong summer sun warms my back. Ants move busily around me. Above me to the north is Mt Shinn, situated deep in the Sierra Nevada alpine landscape. No trails are in sight. Today is a day of solo for me—a time for reflection, self-care, and restoration. I draw strength from this place. I feel a sense of gratitude and privilege to have spent my summers in wild places as a guide, instructor, and now program director working for outdoor programs, specifically leading women's and girls' trips, for more than 20 years. Later today, this alpine meadow will be filled with voices of girls transforming the silence.

It is day seven of a 14-day course with 8th grade girls. We have been rock climbing, canyoneering, camping, and sharing our daily rituals and chores. There has never been a dull moment as the girls navigate their new friendships and roles and take on new challenges. Today, the group of ten girls are backpacking with their instructors to meet me where we will set up basecamp to climb Mt. Shinn—a steep, rocky, semitechnical ramble, requiring route finding, scrambling up a gully and hopping along boulders to reach the final summit of over 3353 m. (11,000 ft).

During my tenure of eight years at GirlVentures, I was curious to know and thus learn what girls appreciated about their all-girl outdoor experience. Instructor teams practiced leadership that emphasized an ethic of care, empathy, and an inclusive learning environment where everyone is heard and seen.

In 2011, I coauthored and published a collaborative study based on three girls' outdoor programs. Data were collected from the program evaluations girls completed at the end of their course. Three themes emerged illustrating "the benefits of these all-girls programs from the girls' point of view: feelings of safety and comfort, increased connection to others, and freedom from stereotypes" (Whittington, et al., 2011, p. 1). Girls also said that boys are a distraction and report that when they are with boys, they are less willing to try new things, show their vulnerability, and express their authentic self. In this all-girl bubble, girls were freer to show their strengths, be in the spotlight, and share their stories of being courageous, strong, and vulnerable.

Now, the girls arrive at the meadow tired and happy to shed the weight of their backpacks. The "leaders of the day" gather the group members to set up camp. Girls take turns leading the group daily. Most girls say the biggest challenge of leading their peers is their fear of being seen as too bossy and possibly not being liked at the end of the day. As girls lead, they are focused on maintaining their peer relationships and leading through a relational lens. In other words, some girls may feel pressured to choose between leadership or friendship.

As part of our curriculum, we ask girls to create a list of messages that they hear from our social construct of what it means to be a girl. They list stereotypes such as passive, cooperative, "good girl," perfect, "doesn't rock the boat," superficial, and dependent. Qualities of a leader, on the other hand, are described as strong, independent thinker, assertive, confident, authentic, and opinionated. For girls to be leaders, it takes a lot of practice in resistance and being bold enough to challenge and to break free from society's expectations and stereotypes. For girls, a lot of unlearning and relearning is required to step out of the social ideal girl box to become an effective leader. Stepping into leadership is often more complex for girls than boys as they navigate society's norms. Our curriculum also includes teaching how to be an ally, so peers support one another in the process.

Handing over leadership so girls feel empowered and can have positive experiences requires a solid plan that includes structure, relevant curriculum and activities, and active coaching from the instructor team. It also requires regular one-to-one time with each student to develop connection and trust. This is a lot in addition to the activity-packed itinerary with rock climbing, backpacking, mountaineering, rappelling, and canyoneering! This work can be exhausting for the instructors and requires commitment to do it well.

Recommendations

Timing is also crucial. It is important to start by having the instructor team model leadership for the first two days before asking the girls to lead. We then set them up for success by following these practices:

♦ Provide the girls clear expectations for their leadership role. Give them a job description.

♦ Be clear about what they can expect from instructors when they are the leaders of the day. One instructor mentors the team of the day. The mentor instructor meets with the leaders of the day the night before to check in and write down and review the next day's plan.

♦ At the end of the day, a mentor instructor meets with leaders of the day to debrief their day before evening meeting when group members share reflections and the leadership is handed to the next team. Create a fun ritual for this leadership change.

♦ Do activities to inspire discussion about leadership. Ask questions such as What is challenging? What do you want from your leaders of the day? How can you support your leaders of the day?

♦ Teach and discuss how to be an ally and how to break stereotypes. This should go beyond being a girl and connect with race, culture, and class. Explore issues of difference.

♦ Teach conflict resolution. Normalize conflict. Connect it with the relational risk of confrontation and its potential for losing friends.

♦ Teach awareness of the relational risk of being a leader— especially when there is a difficult decision to be made or split in group members with a decision. This can be true even if it is as trivial as when to take a break or stop for lunch.

♦ Model what you want to see. Be bold, honest, curious, and vulnerable as a leader too. Set healthy boundaries. Lead with empathy and be open minded.

Back in the city at graduation, the course end celebration, a parent of an assistant instructor who has witnessed a few graduations asks me, "How do you consistently do it?" as she watches the girls beam with newly discovered confidence, pride, and strength in front of their family and friends. "It is the magic of girls and women connecting in and with the mountains," I responded. We challenge

89

ourselves and one another, learn to live together and be allies for one another, and celebrate life. We emphasize empathetic leadership. The community we develop is intentional and inclusive with a compassionate norm. It is one where many girls feel safe and free to step out of gender, racial, and cultural boxes, break stereotypes, and be themselves. In 14 days, we can't help but have some positive long-lasting effect on girls learning to be bold, not bossy, and to confidently step into group leadership.

It is no wonder that this has become my mission—I have been one of those "bossy" girls my whole life! I still get labeled as bossy when I am being assertive or setting a clear boundary. This work has been a parallel process for me. I am still learning, just as many of us are, to bust out of stereotypes and be allies for one another.

References

Roberts, N. S. (1998). *A guide to women's studies in the outdoors: A review of literature and research with annotated bibliography*. Pearson Publishing Solutions.

Sears, E. (1923). Interview with Alma Wagen, first female guide on Mt. Rainier. *American Magazine 95*, 73.

Whittington, A., Mack, E. N., Budbill, N. W., & McKenney, P. (2011). All-girls adventure programmes: What are the benefits? *Journal of Adventure Education and Outdoor Learning, 11*(1), 114.

Throughout most of my journey, Nina Roberts, as a friend and colleague, was one of my most admired models for being bold and courageous and for speaking her truth. Nina also was passionate about women's outdoor programming. She inspired my work with her first publication in the 1990s, "A Guide to Women's Studies in the Outdoors." At that time, in the outdoor experiential education fields, women's outdoor programs were trending. In graduate school, however, I noticed very little published or mention of girl's outdoor programs. That was the beginning of my next career choice and path for the next 20 plus years. Nina's impact continues through the students that she served directly and also through those I have served as well. Her legacy will continue to ripple outward and onward through bold women and girls!

Photo courtesy of Denise Mitten

Reflections on Diversity and Inclusion in AEE

Sanford Tollette

I was born in 1951, and my education in the outdoors began as early as I can remember in rural Arkansas. My family still has property in Tollette, Arkansas that has been in my family for six generations. An ancestor bought himself out of slavery, learned to read and write, purchased the land, and became one of the first post riders. I grew up in the country catching frogs and any other creatures I could find. I was protected by this Black community, and I could be myself. My family has always been a great source of strength and placed great emphasis on education and achieving. If you were doing something positive, you were supported, even if you failed. I learned a commitment to hard work and professional success. My dad had a master's degree in education and doctorate in divinity. My mom had a master's in library science and accomplishments in her own right. I also understood that as a Black man good was never good enough. I have always been driven to over-achieve and struggled to receive recognition.

When I was 11, we moved to Little Rock, and reality kicked me in the face. It was the first time in my life that I encountered White people and the first time I was spat on and experienced racism. My mother taught me about dealing with racism. In graduate school, although she had gotten a 98 on an exam, she did not get an A. When she went to the professor, he said, "I don't give As to colored people." Knowing that there was nothing she could do, she walked away with quiet strength. That's the example I follow. However, there is exhaustion and anger inside. Anger can be a source of strength, but at times suppressed emotions come out.

When I became director of Pfeifer Camp in 1976, I didn't fit most people's stereotype. In Black communities being a teacher, doctor, lawyer, engineer, or architect are professions one aspires to, not a camp director. But my family embraced it because I was doing it. In the White community, people who look like me aren't expected to be the director. Today, I still experience guests arriving at camp who ask me where to find the director. During my 47 years at Pfeifer Camp in a White rural community with a previously all White board of directors, I have experienced challenges, but I have endured, raising over $30,000,000 to support experiential programs for children who normally cannot afford such opportunities. Former campers frequently tell us about their current outdoor experiences and life successes and point to our programs as the root. It is the only camp in Arkansas licensed as a residential childcare facility and boasts successful alumni.

My advice to experiential educators is the importance of knowing the needs of the participants. At Pfeifer Camp, we do adventure AND life and academic skills. Many experiential programs do not address academics. It's important to know how to spell, write a paragraph, and present yourself professionally. If we want to help kids, those are the real life skills.

As a camp director, I was involved with the American Camp Association but found AEE as a place where my nontraditional ideas were accepted and encouraged. It was important to me to be accepted as having a good brand and a creative program, yet I sometimes felt like I had to prove that I was an experiential educator. We had extensive research on our Alternative Classroom Experience (ACE) program, but I had difficulty gaining traction with the AEE research side. But after 40 years, AEE's Dr. Simon Priest published and presented his research on our ACE program with profound results. Time heals.

At the St. Paul, Minnesota, AEE conference, I gave a plenary presentation about the River Rock, which is a metaphorical story about life and the hardships we all experience regardless of our backgrounds. It is about staying committed and eventually succeeding. We all have a journey, and my story is no worse, no less, no better, no more, or no less painful than your story. And who we have become is that beauty in all of us. My parents instilled a passionate belief and commitment to helping other people, especially people who are not being heard and not being represented. One doesn't have to be successful by climbing on top of others.

The diversity and inclusion session at the St. Paul conference gave voice to conversations about women's rights, minority rights, and LGBTQ rights. At Lake Junaluska, NC, NAALA (Native, African, Asian, Latino, and Allies) was created and took off. It gave us, as minorities, a special interest group, a place within the organization to move forward on things that were valuable to us. In that process I met Nina Roberts, Rosario Carelli, Arthur Conquest, Hepsi Barnett, and others. NAALA and the Women's Professional group were dynamic in the health and growth of AEE and were instrumental in gaining representation in AEE.

A high point of my time in AEE was when I was elected to the board of directors in 1994. We were a diverse group—LGBTQ, straight, Black, White, Jewish, Christian, men, women. It was the inclusivity that saved us and allowed us to deal with difficult issues such as having lost incorporation status. Today, I don't see much diversity on the Board, but I do see many participating in different ways. Another high point was when I gave the Kurt Hahn Address (now the Marina Ewald and Kurt Hahn address), with my mother, father, wife, and children in the audience. I was so humbled. The AEE friendships are still here today, even if we haven't seen each other in a long time.

AEE is far from perfect in terms of diversity, equity, and inclusion. While I have seen more minorities involved, AEE is still a very White organization that for whatever reason limits the leadership potential of many people. Specifically, I would love to see more Black people in the industry. It is important for agencies associated with experiential education to allow pathways for minorities to move up the ranks within the agency, including head positions. Nevertheless, AEE provides opportunities for concerns to be voiced. Perhaps there needs to be a stronger effort to voice these concerns beyond AEE and into the larger circle of experiential education, and AEE could provide that pathway.

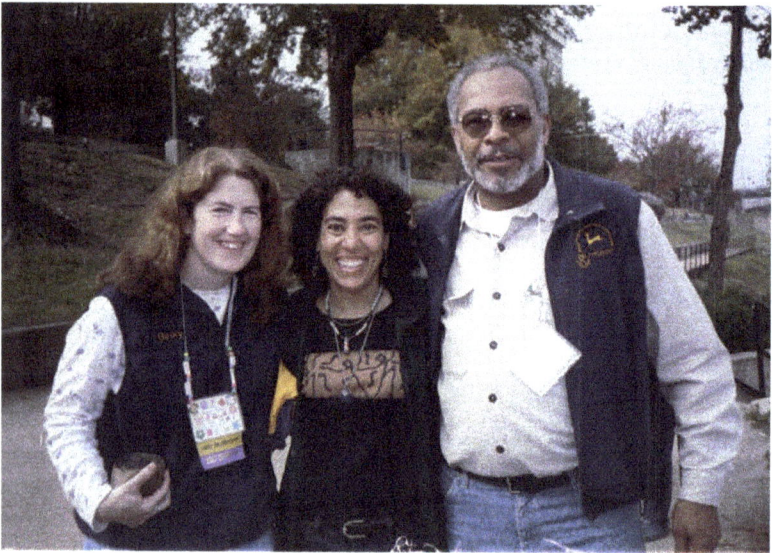

Photo courtesy of the Roberts Family

The Never-Ending Quest for Safety and Belonging

Christine Norton

As a woman in the outdoor field, I have spent my career second guessing myself, experiencing imposter syndrome, people-pleasing, placating, and overcommitting. I used to think these things were just facets of my personality, but I now realize they are also gendered and racialized limitations I've internalized based on patriarchal and White supremacist norms.

I am waking up to the painful reality that gender-based power dynamics exist even when I pretend that they don't. Recent human history as well as my own family and cultural history confirm the existence of these complex and oppressive dynamics and support Koester's (2015) claim that all "gender relations are power relations" (para. 5). When men ignore this, they ignore the male privilege with which they walk through the world. And when women ignore this, they risk denying their authentic selves and not supporting one another.

Recently, a woman-identifying colleague commented that sexism in the outdoor fields is exhausting; I responded, it is more than exhausting. It is threatening. It threatens our sense of self-worth, safety, and belonging, which activates the central nervous system's stress response. This biological stress response has physical and mental health consequences for those being oppressed or threatened. A recent study showed that women who reported at least one act of gender-based harassment or discrimination in the past year were 26% more likely to report psychological distress and depression (Hackett et al., 2019). I have felt the inflammatory effects of sexism from the cortisol response that accompanies gender-based inequities that I experienced growing up, throughout my education, and now in my personal and professional life as an adult woman. In fact, there is evidence that women experience cumulative trauma from gender-based discrimination over the course of their lifetimes (Kucharska, 2018). In particular, Black, Indigenous, and People of Color (BIPOC) women have experienced a combination gender-based and racial trauma that "subjects them to experiences of gendered racial micro- and macro-aggression and racial battle fatigue" (BIPOC Women's Health Network, n.d., para. 2).

To me, the most heartbreaking aspect of all of this is how the burden of proof falls on those who directly experience the trauma of oppression. Many people don't believe women. They want "proof." My emotions as a woman and the ways I literally feel unsafe in my body are not enough. When a woman shows her emotions, she may be labeled "manic" or "overly-emotional," labels I've been called by supposed men allies in this field. Even if a woman provides data, she may still experience gaslighting. Gaslighting is a real and studied psychological phenomenon; it is when people "induce in someone the sense that her reactions, perceptions, memories and/or beliefs are not just mistaken, but utterly without grounds" (Abramson, 2014).

One of my mentors, Dr. Karen Warren (1996), wrote that "barriers to women's involvement and ability to have a voice in the field of experiential education have often been complex, difficult to articulate and cumulative" (p. 3). Despite this difficulty and the very real risk of not being believed or being gaslighted, I share what sexism has looked like for me in the field of outdoor experiential education research and practice—data that come from my lived experience.

During my career as an outdoor educator, adventure therapist, and researcher, some men-identifying colleagues consistently disregarded and therefore disrespected the work I've done. They have attacked my integrity as a researcher, while praising and celebrating men colleagues who have done similar research.

97

Male-identifying peers in this field have benefitted from double-standards based on male privilege and often "mansplain" condescendingly, with little to no curiosity about the thoughts, feelings, or ideas of their women colleagues. On more than one occasion, I have even had personal aspects of my life slanderously dragged into the public arena by men who have bullied me, mocked me, and shamed me, and I have had supposed allies turn on me behind my back. At the very least, I have coyly played along, not wanting to rock the boat. At my worst, I have become dysregulated and lost my ability to "go high when they go low."

The irony is that the more successful I get as a woman in outdoor experiential education, the more invalidated I feel. Even men-identifying allies who seem to be cheering me on have taken credit for my success, competed with me, or have not fully shared their social and professional capital by not inviting me to partner on research or other important projects. I've even had men simply not respond to work I've produced or to my professional emails, letters, or phone calls. Nothing. Rendering me invisible.

I am ashamed to admit that I have rarely stood up for myself in these situations. Instead, I have desperately sought safety and belonging by trying to be one of the guys. On numerous occasions, I have found myself hanging out, sarcastically bantering back and forth in a room full of men. This tendency to want to "fit in with the guys" is not always reflective of authentic connection. Instead, it may be a stress response, shaped by my socialization, that influences me to compensate relationally, when what I should be doing is setting boundaries for myself. I want to move through the world with an ethic of care that prioritizes the importance of human relationships (Gilligan, 1993). However, trying to be relational in the face of misogyny is actually the opposite of caring for myself and others and ends up being a self-sacrificing strategy to fit in and create a false sense of belonging. I should not have to people-please and "be nice" to create safety and belonging while among men.

Personal Strengths and Relational Resources

I grew up in a patriarchal religious environment with a father who believed that men were the head of the household. His worldview about women caused him to encourage me to be demure and attractive. In some ways, I credit him for a lot of who I have become because I developed as a woman in direct opposition to many of the values and gender norms he tried to impose on me. I was an athlete. I became an outdoor educator and adventure therapist. I became a wife and a mother. But I have never derived my entire identity from those roles, valuing my independence and professional identities as well.

In the literature, this is known as positive deviance. Positive deviance is a term used to describe positive norm-departing actions of people who go against the grain to create positive change (Spreitzer & Sonenshein, 2004). By doing the opposite of those around them, they can find new solutions and ways of being that open up more possibilities. For me, it was the ability to create my identity as a strong, independent woman even in the midst of traditional gender role expectations.

Interestingly, it has been my experiences in the outdoors that have engendered this sense of positive deviance. When I used to go camping with my mom on her hunting trips, attended an outdoor leadership school as an adolescent girl, was an Outward Bound student, then instructor, and was an adventure therapist on wilderness expeditions—in many ways, these experiences provided freedom from the expectations of traditional gender roles and focused more on expedition behavior and survival. These experiences have been where I felt the most authentic connection rather than just trying to fit in. These were often equalizing experiences where women intentionally cocreated equitable spaces together.

I have felt great support in these outdoor spaces from women who identified as lesbian and queer, an interesting fact given how bravely many of these women have had to face both sexism and homophobia.

BIPOC women have also compassionately provided support to me in these fields, one in particular helping me apply a racial lens to the exhausting people-pleasing I often engage in with White men. These moments of compassion and insight forged out of oppression were offered to me as alternative ways of seeing the world and have helped me acknowledge the truth about gender-based power dynamics.

A Word About Allies

To the men who have been allies, I see you. You are the ones who listened. Who took me seriously. Who respected my work, even if you disagreed with it. Who never questioned my motives or integrity. You were the ones who shared power, but also didn't leave a leadership vacuum making me do all the work. You were the ones who empathized, and, most of all, you were the ones who listened deeply and acknowledged when I was not valued.

Peggy McIntosh (1988) wrote, "just as whites are carefully taught not to recognize white privilege, men are taught not to recognize male privilege" (p. 91). Therefore, my call to action for men-identifying allies is for acknowledgement, ownership, and empathy: acknowledgement that systemic sexism exists in our field; ownership of male privilege, which exists whether a man considers himself to be a progressive or an ally or even a feminist; and empathy for how painful and scary sexism and oppression are for the person experiencing it and empathy that inspires deep equity listening.

Remember that being an ally is not simply a relational endeavor—it's about ownership of privilege and power sharing as well as holding other men accountable, which is a lot harder than just being nice.

References

Abramson, K. (2014). Turning up the lights on gaslighting. *Philosophical Perspectives*, *28*, 1–30.

BIPOC Women's Health Network. (n.d.) Addressing the intergenerational transmission of trauma in Black women with trauma informed care. https://bipocwomenshealth.com/cultural- resources/african-carribean-black-health/addressing-the-intergenerational- transmission-of-trauma-in-black-women-with-trauma-informed-care/

Gilligan, C. (1993). *In a different voice: Psychological theory and women's development*. Harvard University Press.

Hackett, R. A., Steptoe, A., & Jackson, S. E. (2019). Sex discrimination and mental health in women: A prospective analysis. *Health Psychology*, *38*(11),1014.

Koester, D. (2015). Gender and power: Six links and one big opportunity. DLProg. https://www.dlprog.org/opinions/gender-and-power-six-links-and-one-big-opportunity

Kucharska, J. (2018). Cumulative trauma, gender discrimination and mental health in women: Mediating role of self-esteem. *Journal of Mental Health*, *27*(5), 416–423.

Spreitzer, G. M., & Sonenshein, S. (2004). Toward the construct definition ofpositive deviance. *American Behavioral Scientist*, *47*(6), 828–847.

Stewart, C. (2019). 4 types of power: What are power over; power with; power to and power within? https://sustainingcommunity.wordpress.com/2019/02/01/4-types-of-power/

Warren, K. (1996). The quilt of women's voices. In K. Warren (Ed.), *Women'svoices in experiential education* (pp. 1–5). Kendall/Hunt.

Is the Outdoors Gendered?

Denise Mitten

The history perpetuated in outdoor education, the media (past and present), and hegemonic thinking in Western society contributes to women and other marginalized groups of people being virtually invisible in mainstream outdoor education. This includes women's and other marginalized groups' ways of being as well as their competencies, contributions, and accomplishments.

One classic example is the celebrated history of Kurt Hahn, who cofounded a number of schools including Salem School in 1920 and Outward Bound in 1941. A 2022 Internet search for Hahn reveals no cofounder named for Salem School, although Prince Max von Baden is mentioned as Hahn's benefactor. In Hahn's personal papers, Marina Ewald (a childhood friend of Hahn's) is described by Hahn (1968) as "a cofounder of Salem. She was a partner in all the major decisions—an educator in her own right . . . Her contribution is held in high regard" (p. 1). When Hahn fled to the United Kingdom during the Nazi regime, Ewald remained as director for 50 years. Golo Mann (1990), a student at Salem and later a history professor, describes Ewald as Hahn's educational partner.

Ewald was virtually unknown to outdoor educators until a series of small events were brought to their attention. She was briefly mentioned in Veevers' (2006) master's work, which led me as the 2011 Kurt Hahn addressee at the Association of Experiential Education (AEE) international conference to further research Ewald and highlight her. This led to more people writing about Ewald (Gray et al., 2017). In 2019, the AEE Board formally changed the Kurt Hahn Address to the Marina Ewald & Kurt Hahn Address. More information is now available about Ewald on the AEE Website (aee.org) and the Internet.

Marina Ewald was instrumental in the inception of the expeditionary learning model used by Outward Bound and numerous other outdoor programs as well as expeditionary learning schools. In 1925, Ewald, a geographer, initiated Salem School's first sailing expedition to Finland and Iceland. After this, she advocated using outdoor expeditions as a learning model and incorporated expeditions into the school curriculum. As a result, Hahn (who had never been particularly interested in sailing or outdoor travel) embedded expeditions into his educational endeavors and today we hail him for his vision and inspiration. Ironically, this piece of history—i.e., Ewald's role in the establishing the expeditionary model—had been completely subjugated. Thus, we have a gender-washed asymmetrical (his)story.

I purposefully use the term mainstream outdoor education. Many educators, researchers, and practitioners talk about outdoor fields as homogeneous, not realizing that many Black, Indigenous, and People of Color (BIPOC) communities (e.g., Latino Outdoors, Outdoor Afro, and Project Venture—a program for Native American youth), women's groups (e.g., Adventures in Good Company, Fat Girls Hiking, Wild Women Expeditions, Women in the Wilderness, and Woodswomen, Inc.) and others have different historical influencers and different histories. When talking about outdoor history and leadership, these programs and their practices are often not mentioned. This leads many people to see the outdoor education professions as more homogeneous in practice and histories than they are, while keeping other practices and histories invisible or adopting practices from marginalized groups without giving credit.

Mainstream outdoor education history and practice often emphasizes the role of White male founders and leaders while excluding the contributions and leadership of others. Accurately referring to such history and programming as mainstream, when appropriate, helps people remember that there are organizations and groups of people who methodologically and pedagogically may operate differently than outdoor education organizations influenced by the common narratives about outdoor education history dominated by White men.

Participants and practitioners in outdoor and adventure education receive some level of information about the history of these fields through formal class time as well as informally at conferences and from employing organizations (often on their websites). Typically, White males are given a privileged, often exclusive, level of attention and significance. For example, Kurt Hahn, John Dewey, and Paul Petzoldt are heavily emphasized as "forefathers," while the accomplishments of influential women such as Marina Ewald, Maria Montessori, and Laura Mattoon, to name only a few, are largely unacknowledged. Few people participating in outdoor education learn that Laura Mattoon was an innovator in the field of camping (a critical antecedent of adventure education) and served as the first salaried executive of what is now the American Camping Association (Miranda, 1987). Labeling White men as "forefathers" sets up the history in a patriarchal manner, which then permeates programming. As history is a perspective, it is essential to reclaim a history that celebrates many diverse stories and contributions, including those of People of Color, women, nonbinary people, and more.

I suggested changing the conversation about history as a genealogical to an ecological systems point of view, emphasizing that people from many intellectual and practical niches have contributed to outdoor experiential education fields from their perspectives in their respective areas (Mitten, 2021). Thinking in terms of systems and relationships encourages people to find complementary and contradictory contributions and question dominant paradigms. In an ecological system, seemingly small contributions may be crucial for the whole ecosystem to thrive. A systems view may help open our capacity to value and include more contributions of underrepresented groups—People of Color, women, nonbinary people, people with varying abilities—in our scholarly discussions. Valuing contributions, including people behind the scenes (e.g., as described in the movie Hidden Figures) is a feminist perspective that reinforces a paradigm of an ecology of relationships. Engaging more voices and diversity redistributes power and access. Further, the need to decolonize outdoor education fields has been noted (Root, 2010; Tuck, McKenzie, & McCoy, 2014). Using an ecological and systems analysis when talking about contributions and history as well as current voices could contribute to decolonizing outdoor education fields.

In addition to People of Color, women, nonbinary people, and others being washed from history, scholars and others tend to generalize research findings that then become the fabric of outdoor fields. For example, I have read many articles that begin with a premise that the outdoors is gendered male or masculine or the authors might say the outdoors is a masculine space. Mainstream media validates or reinforces that many men go into the outdoors to achieve feats, including conquering mountains, rivers, and other environments, often referred to as adversaries (Mayer, 2017). In mainstream outdoor learning, numerous authors (of many genders) have identified this field as primarily catering to men. Even today mainstream outdoor learning is primarily dominated by men in leadership (Rogers & Rose, 2019). Referring to the outdoors as male space dominated by men fails to recognize that many people have learned about the outdoors and participated in outdoor programming activities outside mainstream outdoor programming.

In my work, I have found that I think differently than many people in mainstream outdoor learning, which contributes to why I do not feel that I belong in mainstream outdoor and adventure education. Growing up, I experienced the outdoors as a place for women and girls. As a child, I ran around outdoors at home and at Girl Scout camp, and later with my Girl Scout troop. I experienced strong women, and lots of fun hiking, backpacking, sailing, and generally living outdoors. I grew up seeing outdoor learning as a space welcoming to girls and women. It also meant that I did not see the outdoors as a masculine space or gendered male. I experienced the outdoors as nurturing and sometimes challenging.

I and other girls and women were probably performing gender as girls and women. We were being outdoors in ways that seem compatible with who we were and many of those attributes could be labeled as feminine (e.g., using inclusive leadership, valuing emotional needs, and pacing a trip that allows for relationship building with other people, nature, and self). This meant we performed what might be typified as gender stereotypic behavior.

In 1969, as a CIT (Counselor in Training) at a Girl Scout camp, I learned more accurate information about group development and group dynamics than I was taught in formal teaching in courses about outdoor leadership. What I learned as a CIT and through observation and experience in my formative years included being attentive and caring to group members, including their social, emotional, spiritual, and physical needs. I was taught and it was modeled to be inclusive, which meant, among other things, that not everyone had to carry the same physical weight and people could contribute to the well-being of the community in many ways. Girls and women did not need to be changed or taught to be good enough to adventure in the outdoors. Women's strengths were assets to programs. Compassionate and caring leadership (now often labeled trauma-informed leadership) based on an ethic of care (Noddings, 2012) and developmental needs were taught and practiced. The science of compassion has since been "rediscovered" and more mainstream leadership teachings now are embracing compassionate leadership.

As a person from working-poor and working-class parents, I did not feel out of place at my camp—I felt included and that I belonged. In the 1960s and 70s, there was not an emphasis on the latest gear. Therefore, I did not need expensive outdoor gear to fit in.

My early experiences translate into how I lead and facilitate groups of people in outdoor spaces. Often, the men around me said above all a leader should treat everyone the same, which would be fair. On one coed summer course, this difference showed during an activity where students had to shoot a tied-up lamb, butcher it, roast it, and eat it. One vegetarian student asked not to participate because she did not believe in killing animals even for meat; I concurred with her nonparticipation. When staff debriefed the course, I was told that I should have treated everyone fairly and equally and made her participate. That did not make sense to me; I could not figure out why they saw making everybody participate as fair. Making her participate in any way could have been traumatizing and perhaps spiritually damaging. Now I realize it was our difference in leadership training and socialization.

Rogers and Rose (2019) found that the women outdoor leaders they interviewed resonated with the experiences and scholarship that questioned masculine norms in outdoor education. Their work confirmed what Henderson (1996) found: "Female values, not traditionally linked with [mainstream] leadership were associated with a priority on form and harmony; concern for people, unity, spirituality, a desire to help and care for others, and a concern for beauty and creative expression" (pp. 109– 110). These leadership practices and outdoor pedagogy inspired by women mimic egalitarian cultures before the Bronze Age (Gimbutas & Marler, 1991). Many marginalized groups have practiced this type of leadership for more than a century (Mitten & Woodruff, 2010).

These practices, which marginalized groups have historically used and some mainstream outdoor educators now use, help create trip environments that are nurturing emotionally, socially, spiritually, and physically. These practices include offering choice in participation (e.g., participation by choice, challenge by choice), traveling at a pace that encourages healthy relationships with others and nature and allows time for participants to build competencies, and helping participants learn about the natural environments where they travel. Leaders' role modeling and teaching participants to value other beings and systems in natural environments for their own sake and not using nature as a means to an end (e.g., not creating situations to take risks and prove dominance over nature) is crucial. These trip environments in turn help people feel a sense of belonging, which increase opportunities for learning and growth.

Give credit where credit is due. Acknowledging the competencies, contributions, and accomplishments of women, nonbinary people, BIPOC people and communities, differently abled people, and other marginalized communities historically and currently helps create more inclusive outdoor experiential education. This includes researching and citing scholars from marginalized communities.

References

Hahn, K. (1968, August 14). [Letter to Skidelsky]. Gordonstoun School Archive, Gordonstoun School, Elgin, Moray, Scotland.

Henderson, K. (1996). Women and the outdoors: Toward spiritual empowerment. In K. Warren (Ed.) *Women's voices in experiential education* (pp. 193–202). Kendall Hunt.

Gimbutas, M. and Marler, J. (1991). The civilization of the goddess: *The worldof old Europe.* Harper.

Gray, T., Mitten, D., Loeffler, TA, Allen-Craig, S., & Carpenter, C. (2017). Defining moments: An examination of the gender divide in women's contribution to outdoor education. *Research in Outdoor Education 15,* 47–71.

Mann, G. (1990). *Reminiscences and reflections: Growing up in Germany.* Faber & Faber.

Mayer, B. (2017). The lived experiences of whitewater kayakers: A phenomenological exploration. (Publication No. 10689210) [master's thesis Prescott College]. ProQuest Dissertations Publishing.

Mitten, D. (2021). Critical perspectives on outdoor therapy practices. In N. J.Harper and W.W. Dobud, (Eds.), *Outdoor therapies: An introduction to practices, possibilities, and critical perspectives* (pp. 175–187). Routledge.

Mitten, D. & Woodruff, S. (2010). Women's adventure history and education programming in the United States favors friluftsliv. *Norwegian Journal of Friluftsliv.* Available at http://norwegianjournaloffriluftsliv.com/doc/212010.pdf

Miranda, W. (1987). The genteel radicals. *Camping Magazine, 59*(4), 12.

Nodding, N. (2012). The caring relation in teaching. *Oxford Review of Education, 38*(6), 771–781.

Rogers, E. B., & Rose, J. (2019). A critical exploration of women's genderedexperiences in outdoor leadership. *Journal of Experiential Education, 42*(1),37–50.

Root, E. (2010). This land is our land? This land is your land: The decolonizing journeys of white outdoor environmental educators. *Canadian Journal of Environmental Education, 15*, 103–119.

Tuck, E., McKenzie, M., & McCoy, K. (2014). Land education: Indigenous, post-colonial, and decolonizing perspectives on place and environmental education research. *Environmental Education Research, 20*(1), 1–23.

Veevers, N.J. (2006). Your disability is your opportunity: A historical study of Kurt Hahn focusing on the early development of outdoor activities. [Master'sdissertation, University of Edinburgh Moray House School of Education].

Photo courtesy of Sue Tracy, All Out Adventures

Overcoming "Not Enough": A Pathway to Inclusivity

Lise Brown

I was raised in Winnipeg, on Treaty One Territory, by my mom and dad. I'm a little sister, an auntie, a mama to my son Tian, and an owner and facilitator at Momenta, Inc. I work in the areas of adventure therapy, positive youth development, outdoor education, and forest school. For me, the natural world has been a constant—my favorite place to be. It has also been my friend, mentor, teacher, and a coparent to me.

In my profession, adventure education, I sometimes refer to three zones:

- the comfort zone is easy, relaxed, and predictable.

- the danger zone is stressful, fearful, frustrating, and exhausting.

- the stretch zone is fun, challenging, alive, exhilarating, and dreamy.

During my early years of leading outdoor adventures, I was in the stretch zone a lot, and it felt awesome. I found that I was strong, confident, talented, and resilient. I had many varied experiences, with hundreds of days in the field. But despite all this, there was something missing for me. I noticed a feeling of not being good enough, of not owning gear that was good enough, of not measuring up to my male coguides. I noticed that everyone who taught me about leading outdoor adventures were men, and none of those leaders acknowledged the land we adventured on or the colonial and Indigenous history of that land.

In 2006, I found myself at an Association for Experiential Education conference where I met a group of women who led with

111

humility, who were bad ass outdoor educators, and who considered feminism, social justice, and land justice in the field. My hesitancies about outdoor adventure education were validated for the first time in my career. Our collective experiences wove a predictable storyline about how the outdoor adventure industry does not address inclusivity and we continue to witness that today:

- It does not adequately acknowledge (and protect) ancestral lands.

- It is led primarily by White males.

- It has numerous barriers to participation by marginalized populations that are not experienced by White males.

These inclusion problems in the outdoor adventure industry require leaders to dream up something better. I left that conference with the confidence to think differently. I was more committed to creating outdoor adventures that reduced barriers and engaged humbly with the land, and to addressing stories about discrimination and the lack of inclusion.

That same year, Sara Harrison and I cocreated Momenta. Sara is a woman I had guided a few trips with and who noticed the same things I did. Sara and I knew that if we could work and play with sensitivity in the stretch zone for participants, we could spark a love for outdoor adventures and leave them feeling confident and wanting more. We came up with the name Momenta, which is the feminine plural of momentum, and we picked a set of values that we wanted to demonstrate in our leadership.

WE HAVE FUN. We are engaging, adventurous, and passionate. At Momenta, we invite people to stretch their limits outdoors. It's challenging, it's getting folks into the stretch zone, and it has to be fun. Laughter, joy, and play are top priorities.

WE TAKE CARE OF EACH OTHER. We are approachable, we are mentors, we are community. We create a safe environment for participants and encourage them to do their best to practice caring relationships with one another. We act as allies for one another and leave space for everyone.

WE ARE RESPECTFUL. We model inclusion, we lead with humility, we are strengths focused. This value is one of the Seven Sacred Laws that reminds our participants and staff that we have been taught through reciprocal relationships to respect each other and the land.

WE JOIN IN. We create a space where people can authentically join conversations, therapy, activities, and outdoor adventures. Joining in must be a choice; that is, we must be ready to create experiences where people can freely join in, open to the different ways that people join in, and curious during moments when some feel that they can't join in.

WE ARE SAFE. We are professional, we are guided by best practice, we have good judgment. To truly offer safe, professional outdoor adventures, a leader has a lot to think about for their own and the participants' physical, emotional, social, and spiritual safety.

Our values are at the heart of our organization. For 17 years they have grounded our work and kept our team providing inclusive programs in the outdoor adventure industry. One of the ways that supports us at Momenta to do this has been our B Corp certification that holds us to "the highest standards of verified social and environmental performance, public transparency and legal accountability." Within our B Corp goals, we have prioritized understanding colonial history and the original intentions of the treaties, adhering to ethical employment policies to diversify the field and increase access to outdoor adventures. Our B Corp goals, along with our five values, have led to a place of work and play that continues to foster strengths and sustain our community. I don't know a lot of other organizations that prioritize having fun.

In the early 2000s, my business partner, Sara, and I spent a lot of time traveling to different communities and camps to deliver programming. One day we were in a truck in Northern Manitoba, and in a spiral of negativity. We were having a bumpy adventure. I remember we were looking at each other and knowing that we could do better. So, we made a commitment to not complain and instead to be solution focused, to keep having fun, and to not miss out on the adventurous career we had chosen.

That moment of choosing to have fun has stuck with me. It was a choice to be strengths focused, to sustain each other, and to stay passionate, engaged, and adventurous in the face of the challenges we'd set out to tackle. Without intentionally choosing to have fun, I'm not sure we'd still be here. More than that, by asking ourselves, "is everyone having fun?" we stay attuned to what might be missing in someone else's adventure.

If we as outdoor adventure educators want to do better as an industry, we need to notice when the experiences that we are providing are working. At Momenta, it starts with this question. Are we all having fun? Are participants playing in the stretch zone of the experiences that are provided? Are we? Pushing the limits of this industry is playful, passionate work. It doesn't always follow the most comfortable or predictable path. Having fun keeps us imagining and moving forward so that we remain engaged in the work that has yet to be done.

We Still Have Work to Do

Mary Breunig

Historically, outdoor trips and outdoor professions have been deeply segregated by gender, race, ethnicity, socio-economic status, and ability as well as other intersectional identities (Warren, et al., 2013). Two examples are included in this paper to highlight these ongoing challenges followed by a call to action to acknowledge and further consider some of these historical injustices.

In April 2022, I volunteered for a Wilderness Inquiry (WI) Canoemobile outing. WI provides equitable access to the outdoors for people of all ages, backgrounds, and abilities. The Minneapolis-based organization started as an initiative to demonstrate that people with disabilities could enjoy the wilderness with little to no accommodations other than positive attitudes and a collective group effort. WI's Canoemobile is a "floating classroom" that offers students the opportunity to paddle their local, urban waterways in 24-foot Voyageur canoes to learn about science, history, geography, and culture. As I paddled with sixth grade students on the Consumnes River in California, one student of color turned around in his seat and said, "I see that all the instructors are White, are any of you racist?"

This group was 90% students of color with Spanish as their first language. The WI instructors were all White, young, pale-skinned Midwesterners. The perceptive student recognized a gap between the written mission of this organization and the lack of representative diversity of its outdoor instructors.

Another example that affects diversity, equity, inclusion, and belonging (DEIB) in experiential education programs is how the media portrays adventurers. Recently, I wrote about a young

115

explorer named Colin O'Brady who was featured on the popular United States NBC Today morning show. Colin was a member of a team of six rowers who crossed the Drake Passage and became the first known person to reach the South Pole unassisted via human-powered watercraft (George, 2020). In addition to that extraordinary feat (dubbed "The Impossible Row"), O'Brady had previously accomplished the Explorer's Grand Slam—reaching both the North and South Poles and setting speed records for ascents of the highest peak on each of the seven continents (Stulberg, 2016). He did this despite being told he may not walk again after a 2008 backpacking accident left him with a traumatic brain injury.

This type of epic adventure story, focused on a (White) man "conquering the wilderness" and overcoming adversity mimics many of the great adventure narratives of North American and Western European lore (Breunig, 2020) such as Magellan's circumnavigation around the world, Shackleton's voyage to the South Pole, Mallory's purported summit of Everest, and other achievements deemed noteworthy.

These traditional historical and media narratives of White men conquering nature are increasingly recognized as problematic, particularly by women and Indigenous people who seek an integrated rather than an adversarial relationship with the natural environment (Gray & Mitten, 2018) and who demand that outdoor enthusiasts explicitly grapple with male settler colonialism (Newberry, 2012). The forced relocation of Indigenous peoples from their homelands in North America to develop wilderness areas for public recreational consumption by wealthy male European immigrants demands attention (Laurendeau, 2020; Lowan-Trudeau, 2017) as does the marginalization of perspectives of Black, Indigenous, and People of Color (BIPOC), whose individual experiences and collective memories are not represented in predominantly male Euro-centric discourse (Finney, 2014). Further, interpretations of concepts such as challenge, adventure, and risk and the hegemonic premise that physically ambitious outdoor adventures engender participant growth have been scrutinized in the outdoor adventure and leisure fields and contested by those concerned about the ways these perspectives can (re)produce ableism, racism, classism, sexism, heterosexism, and sizeism (Warren & Breunig, 2019).

While conceptually easy to understand, these examples create barriers to DEIB. Rather than use these two narratives and examples to point out ongoing deficits and challenges, I encourage readers to use them as a call to action.

Action Steps

- Continue to develop social justice literacy and increase self-awareness relevant to conscious and unconscious biases (see, for example, https://www.titlemax.com/discovery-center/lifestyle/50-cognitive-biases-to-be-aware-of-so-you-can-be-the-very-best-version-of-you/

- Unpack your backpack of privilege (Warren, 2009) relevant to your own OEE hegemonic privilege(s).

- Take decolonization steps in your program. List a minimum of five and track progress meticulously setting actionable goals and assessing short- and long-term efficacy and success.

- Be a social justice advocate and work for greater DEIB.

- Amplify BIPOC voices relevant to your professional communities of practice and/or scholarship.

References

Breunig, M. (2020). Slow nature-focused leisure in the days of COVID-19: Repressive myths, social (in)justice, and hope. Invited paper for Special Issueof *Annals of Leisure Research*. https://doi.org/10.1080/11745398.2020.1859390

Discovery Center. https://www.titlemax.com/discovery-center/lifestyle/50-cognitive-biases-to-be-aware-of-so-you-can-be-the-very-best-version-of-you/

Finney, C. (2014). *Black faces, white spaces: Reimagining the relationship of African Americans to the great outdoors*. University of North Carolina Press.

George, R. (2020, January 14). The Today Show. NBC.

Gray, T., & Mitten, D. (Eds). (2018). *The Palgrave international handbook of women and outdoor learning*. Palgrave Macmillan.

Laurendeau, J. 2020. "Easy Ones": Outdoor recreation, the wilderness ideal,and complicating settler mobility. *Sociology of Sport Journal Advance* online. https://doi:10.1123/ssj.2019-0128

Lowan-Trudeau, G. (2017). Gateway to understanding: Indigenous ecological activism and education in urban, rural, and remote contexts. *Cultural Studies of Science Education*, *12*(1), 119–128.

Newberry, L. (2012). Canoe pedagogy and colonial history: Exploring contested spaces of outdoor environmental education. *Canadian Journal of Environmental Education 17*, 30–45.

Stulberg, B. (2016). How did Colin O'Brady shatter an absolutely insane endurance and adventure record? *Outside*. https://www.outsideonline.com/health/training-performance/how-did-colin-obrady-shatter-absolutely-insane-endurance-and-adventure-record/

Warren, K. (2009). Introduction to social justice in outdoor adventure education. In R. H. Stremba & C. Bisson (Eds.). *Teaching adventure education theory: Best practices* (pp. 221–232). Human Kinetics.

Warren, K., & Breunig, M. (2019). Inclusion and social justice in outdoor education. *Encyclopedia of Teacher Education*. Advance online publication. https://doi.org/10.1007/978-981-13-1179-6_366-1

Warren, K., Roberts, N., Breunig, M., Alvarez, A. (2013). Social justice in outdoor experiential education: A state of knowledge review. *Journal*

of Experiential Education, 37(1), 89–103. https://doi.org/
10.1177/1053825913518898

Photo courtesy of Callie Auman

Is Distinguished What We Really Seek?

Anita R. Tucker

Distinguished Researcher

Starting early in my career as a researcher focusing on documenting the process and outcomes of adventure therapy, I remember being really excited when in 2010, the Association for Experiential Education (AEE) created the Distinguished Researcher Award. Qualifications include AEE membership, important research contributions, a diversity of publication and presentation outlets particularly those that are refereed, creative and innovative impacts to research within the experiential education community, the presence of awards, keynotes, grants, etc. that speak to a research presence, and a minimum of ten years involvement in research (AEE, 2022). In short, this award is given in "recognition of exemplary research productivity and visibility in the fields of Experiential Education" (AEE, 2022, ¶ 1). I was thrilled that the organization that I loved was finally formalizing the importance of research in moving these fields forward. In fact, AEE is the place that I found my professional family—colleagues who empower me, keep me going when things get hard, and remind me that the work we do is ultimately not for ourselves, but for the participants or the clients with whom we work as well as the planet. As an AEE member and volunteer leader, seeing research supported was exciting. I was even more honored when I received the award in 2016.

Distinguished

However, I wrestle with this term *distinguished*. Am I distinguished? Do I want to be distinguished and how is it that this word is important to me in the first place? According to Google's English dictionary, which is provided by their Oxford Languages

Dictionary (2022), distinguished means "successful, authoritative, and commanding great respect." Merriam Webster (2022) defines distinguished as "marked by eminence, distinction or excellence." While I admit I have strived for excellence in my work and my life, words included in the definition such as "commanding," "authoritative," and "eminence" gave me a moment of pause. These definitions seem to be hyper-masculine and to focus on power over. To be distinguished must I be commanding and authoritative and exert power over others?

Who Decides?

Before I was recognized for this award, I remember attending the annual 2014 AEE International Conference in Chattanooga, TN and listening to the Chair of the Council on Research Evaluation (CORE) talk about the importance of supporting research and needing nominations for the Distinguished Researcher Award, as there was no recipient that year. I was shocked to hear this, and all I could think about was the amazing scholars, especially women scholars, who had mentored me through AEE. At that point, only men had won. I asked a White male colleague, who had won the award and was on the award committee why no one had won the award. He said none of the current nominees met the qualifications of both 10 years of publishing and had enough peer reviewed publications. To which I said, "that is impossible, what about [a woman scholar who was quite a leader in the field]? To which he responded, "She is not a real scholar, not like you" (she did not in his opinion have enough peer reviewed publications). Then he proceeded to walk away, while I stood there in shock and frustration. Although this was not my first experience with being gaslighted, it was one of the most memorable.

Gaslighting

The Newport Institute (2021) defines gaslighting as a form of "psychological manipulation in which an individual attempts to sow self-doubt and confusion in another. Gaslighters are seeking to gain power and control over the other person by distorting reality and forcing them to question their own judgment and intuition" (¶ 4). At that moment in 2014, I was told by a well-respected male colleague and friend who I looked up to, that my understanding of scholarship was faulty and my esteem for my woman colleague was unfounded. This gaslighting was done, in the guise of a compliment to me to try to hide the manipulation and convey that he was my ally, which he was not.

Let me share the facts. This woman colleague had written two books, authored 11 book chapters, published over 25 scholarly manuscripts, and mentored over 60 masters and PhD students. In addition, she had been instrumental in chairing AEE's Symposium for Experiential Education Research (SEER), was a member of the editorial board for the *Journal of Experiential Education*, had 30 years of research experience, and was leading voice in looking at the challenges of being a woman in the outdoors and experiential education fields. Clearly, she deserved the award in contrast to a current award recipient, who had edited one book, had few peer reviewed publications, and had engaged in research for less than ten years! What was it? Was she not "authoritative" or "commanding" enough to be considered distinguished? Or was it simply that she was a woman who had spoken up to power so now she was not to be recognized.

Clarity

In all honesty, it took me longer than it should have to see—really see—how dominant the White male narrative of success is throughout the field of experiential education. As a social worker, I knew this played out daily across all settings of our client's lives, so why did I think our fields would be immune? Even now, being a woman in this field is exhausting, especially as I have become more accomplished and gained more influence. Despite my accomplishments, I have been reminded time and time again how my accomplishments are largely due to my male peers' discovery of me and launching of my career. According to their narrative, they are responsible for my success, and I should be grateful. They forget that for the first three years of my academic career, many would not collaborate with me. It was not until I found a group of women collaborators and we built our own path that I was able to fully contribute to the field. My experience is similar to other scholars such as Sandy Newes, Christine Norton, Karen Warren, Denise Mitten, TA Loeffler, Tonia Gray, Rita Yerkes, Deb Sugerman, and the late Nina Roberts.

Backlash

As women, our accomplishments are a threat to the male narrative and the power men wield in deciding who gets awards, who gets recognized, and who by their standards is deserving. Hence, a backlash ensues (Williamson, 2020). In the past few years, my research and that of my colleagues has publicly been criticized by White males of promoting "epistemological violence," by using "worrying" methodology and having a "lack of transparency." There have been personal jabs surrounding the ethics of women researchers as violating "best practices" and having "conflicts of interest." There have been overarching comments that research in adventure therapy is "nascent" at best, while much of that research in the past 10 years has been conducted by women.

Research has grown exponentially due to the hard work of practitioners in the field willing to be vulnerable and partner with researchers, while managing the difficult task of conducting research and running complex therapeutic programs. I am left to wonder if these accusations are just the behavior of male researchers who believe in their "authority" and "eminence"? In fact, this practice of "rankism" or putting others down is common in both racism and sexism (Fuller, 2020). Fuller (2020) noted that we put others down to give us an advantage, "If we can handicap or eliminate the competition, we improve our chances of coming away with the spoils" (¶14). Instead of putting others down, I prefer to work collaboratively and respectfully as researchers and practitioners, even if I see a need to expand on or even challenge another's research work.

Change

I want to be clear. This is not a sob story or story of self-pity. I recognize the privilege I have as a cisgender, heterosexual Christian woman, and the privilege given by my class and education that has granted me access to a PhD and engagement in research. Although it can be exhausting to be a woman, I still have a seat at many tables, while my colleagues of color and LGBTQIA2+ peers are mostly overlooked or not invited. AEE members, especially those of us with privilege due to gender and/ or race, need to change our focus and really do the work, the messy, uncomfortable, and scary work of change.

Most of all, we need to invite others to tell their stories, provide seats at the table, and then get out of the way so those voices can be really heard. We need to learn to be more curious than critical of others, yet analytical of ourselves, to be more collaborative than competitive, and more inviting of difficult dialogue; then, and only then, may there be room for change.

References

Association for Experiential Education (2022). *Awards and honors.* https://www.aee.org/awards-and-honors

Fuller, R. W. (2010). What is rankism and why do we "do" it?https://www.psychologytoday.com/us/blog/somebodies-and-nobodies/201002/what-is-rankism-and-why-do-we-do-it

Google Dictionary - Oxford Languages (2022). *Dictionary*. Distinguished. https://www.google.com/search?q=distinguished+meaning+dictionary&oq=distinguished+meaning+dictionary&aqs=chrome..69i57j0i22i30l7j0i390l2.12232j1j7&sourceid=chrome&ie=UTF-

Merriam Webster (2022). Dictionary. Distinguished. https://www.merriam-webster.com/dictionary/distinguished?utm_campaign=sd&utm_medium=serp&utm_source=jsonld

Newport Institute (2021). How to tell if someone is gaslighting you? https://www.newportinstitute.com/resources/mental-health/what_is_gaslighting_abuse/

Williamson, S. (2020). Backlash, gender fatigue and organisational change: AIRAANZ 2019 presidential address. *Labor and Industry*, *30*. https://doi.org/10.1080/10301763.2019.1677202 https://www.tandfonline.com/doi/full/10.1080/10301763.2019.1677202

Photo courtesy of Robbie Francis

When Actions Speak Louder Than a Mission Statement: Personal Reflection on Diversity, Inclusion, Equity, and Sense of Belonging

Tanya Rao

I grew up in a big city with limited access to wilderness areas and outdoor recreation. I was 19 years old when I went on my first camping and rock climbing trip with the Outdoor Club at my university in Virginia. My love of nature was further cultivated on an independent backpacking trip around the world in my mid-20s; I was drawn to adventure recreation opportunities in faraway wild places rather than to cultural or city tours. In all these explorations, I never once questioned my sense of belonging in the wilderness even though I was rarely in company of people who looked like me. This sort of travel seemed like such a natural fit for my own curious and adventurous personality. For context, I am a South Asian woman who grew up in Bangalore, India and immigrated to the United States in my late teens for educational pursuits.

In 2012, I had the opportunity to take the NOLS Rocky Mountain Outdoor Educator course. I had recently changed careers from being a software engineer in the financial industry to pursuing my passion for adventure recreation through experiential education. I was very excited to take this course and build my outdoor leadership skills through such a renowned institution. The course challenged and helped me grow in so many ways, but most importantly it helped me understand firsthand how social injustices play out in the outdoor field. When I started my graduate program in the Recreation, Parks & Tourism Department at San Francisco State University, I was assigned to work with Dr. Nina Roberts as my advisor. Dr. Roberts was an esteemed educator, researcher, and passionate activist for social and environmental justice in the outdoor profession. It was at our first meeting that I was made acutely aware of my role and responsibility as a woman of color in the field of outdoor recreation. For the first time, I realized that my skin color and cultural history played an important role in defining my (and others') outdoor experiences.

NOLS is undoubtedly a leader and role model for many outdoor organizations in the field. According to their website, NOLS is "committed to creating and fostering environments that are welcoming, equitable, and inclusive for all of our past, present, and future students, instructors and staff" (NOLS, 2022). This is a fundamental requirement for outdoor organizations in today's world, and at the time I took the Outdoor Educator course, the Diversity and Inclusion Manager was a woman of South Asian descent. It seemed that they were following through on their stated diversity commitment. Yet, on my course I found myself to be the only Person of Color among a group of 14 people (11 participants and three instructors). There were more women-identifying members than men-identifying members in the group; however, the dominant leadership style and attitude was one that valued able-bodied, outspoken, and conforming personality traits.

How did these factors influence the outcome of my experience? First, the physical demands of the course put me in my challenge zone—the high altitude, heavy pack weight, and off-trail terrain were completely different from any of my previous multi-day backpacking experiences. As the last person stumbling into camp on our very first day, this created some presumptions among the more able-bodied members of the group. Add to this the intersectionality of gender and race and ethnicity stereotypes, I found myself doubting my own ability and sense of belonging on this course. Nevertheless, I was determined to step into my learning zone and put in my best efforts.

Over the 21-day long course, we students were divided into three tent and hike groups and each participant had the opportunity to be "leader of the day" with tasks such as navigation, course setting, activity planning, and group management. On my days as leader, I was faced with multiple challenges. The first day involved impassable terrain with the instructors intervening to help us renavigate. Additionally, I got my foot stuck between two big boulders leading to a moment of panic and potential helicopter evacuation. Luckily, it was not a major injury and after a well executed wilderness rescue by my fellow participants, I was able to limp the rest of the way to camp. I was physically fine, but it was a crushing blow to my self-confidence and establishing my competence among the group.

The second instance as a leader involved having to be in charge of reassigning our tent and cook groups for the final leg of our expedition. I took a democratic approach and asked for everyone to tell me their preferred group assignments. However, this approach backfired as some social cliques had formed and there was a clear segregation of folks who were deemed "misfits." I wished to create a more balanced group dynamic, so I made the executive decision to form my own group assignments, while considering requests where possible. This was not received well by a few and led to a mutiny of sorts. The instructors had to intervene, again, and tried to resolve the conflict in a large circle group share. This incident left me even more vulnerable and unwelcome as a leader. I am sure that if the decision was made by a White able-bodied heterosexual man, it would have not been questioned or challenged in the same manner. Clouded in my own world of self-doubt, I did not have the courage or support to raise the issue of gender and race that might have led to unconscious bias.

So, what did I learn on this course? I learned a lot of technical outdoor skills, such as off-trail navigation, wilderness risk management, practicing Leave No Trace principles, weather and food planning, and other wilderness leadership "know-hows." I also learned how social and group dynamics play a significant role in the outcomes of these outdoor experiences. As an experiential educator and expedition leader, it is equally important to understand the psychological outcomes of a course as much as (or even more than) the technical skill development.

Despite the challenges, I received an "A-" for overall performance on this course with the instructor evaluation detailing that I "showed strength of self-awareness during adversity both with the physical environment especially when (injured) and during difficult community discussions & decisions." This gave me a boost in confidence, but I was still unable to address the role my gender and ethnicity had on the perceived unconscious bias of my instructors and fellow students.

I was able to process the psychological impact of the experience in more depth with my mentor, Dr. Nina Roberts, who assured me of my inherent competence as an outdoor leader and encouraged me to use my experience and cultural perspective as a learning tool in my own work. I have led multiple youth and women's backpacking trips where I was able to bring a multicultural leadership approach to create an inclusive, safe, and welcoming environment for all. My experience at NOLS was more than a decade ago, and there have been changes with diversity, equity, and inclusion (DEI) initiatives in the outdoor industry. Yes, there has been increased visible participation of People of Color over the years. Yes, there are more organizations by and for People of Color (e.g., Outdoor Afro, Latino Outdoors, PGM One, Melanin Base Camp). There is even a social media hashtag, #DiversifyOutdoors, amplifying the effort. However, there is still more to do and these efforts are a continuum. Based on my experience and research in the field, here are some recommendations for cultivating a socially just and equitable environment in the outdoors.

Recommendations

* **Diversity at all Levels** - A research study of women of color educators showed that role models play a vital role in creating a welcoming and inclusive environment (Rao & Roberts, 2017). Organizations that take a top-down approach, with diversity represented in their senior management and board of directors, show their commitment to social justice and pave the path for future generations. As an educator, hold your leaders accountable to reach the institution's DEI goals.

* **Cultivate Empathy** - Understanding the cultural influences on outdoor experiences for People of Color is a complex endeavor. It involves the interplay of race/ethnicity and gender issues, socialization, and historical access to the outdoors. Seek out reflections of shared outdoor experiences from people of different backgrounds. Examine what was similar and what was different. In understanding how cultural ideologies shape our outdoor experience, outdoor educators can allow for different outcomes within the same group of people or course.

* **See Something, Say Something** - This seems like an obvious recommendation, yet it is difficult to talk about uncomfortable or sensitive topics in group settings. This should be addressed in cultural competency training for outdoor educators and added as a core skill development area for outdoor educator trainings. The topic of race and ethnicity never came up on my NOLS course, and I seemed to be the only one acutely aware of the lack of representation. It would have benefited the entire group greatly if the course instructors had acknowledged it in some manner and provided a framework on how to support

each other given different abilities and recreation histories in the field. In my opinion, this would have reduced the unconscious bias that permeated our entire course experience.

Conclusion

The current perspective of being "inclusive" still feels like an elitist notion of letting diverse people "in" to an already existing and acceptable environment. I encourage taking a more expansive approach of examining different perspectives of shared outdoor experiences and finding ways of commonality and connection. To be truly welcoming and equitable, one must first understand what it feels like to be different.

References

NOLS (2022). Diversity and inclusion plan 2020. https://issuu.com/nols.edu/docs/2020-diversity-and_inclusion-plan.

Rao, T. & Roberts, N.S. (2018). Voices of women of colour: Dreaming of an inclusive outdoor leadership environment. In T. Gray & D. Mitten (Eds.). *The Palgrave international handbook of women and outdoor learning* (pp.815–835). Palgrave Macmillan.

Photo courtesy of Outward Bound Adventures

Reflections on Social Justice

Dan Garvey

I am delighted and honored to be asked to contribute my thoughts about the broad topic of justice, equity, and inclusion in outdoor experiential education, identifying as a White cisgender man. I am also a bit nervous because the request has been made for all of us to share our "personal stories." I am very comfortable writing on the topic of experiential education and have authored articles and books on this subject. I'm less comfortable and completely inexperienced sharing my personal journey. I believe my life experiences have helped me understand the insidious cost of injustice and the potential damaging effects it can have on our resilience and capacity to ride out the inevitable troubles we face.

When I was 29, I was diagnosed with multiple sclerosis. At the time of my diagnosis, I was almost excessively active—racing bicycles, mountaineering, and doing almost any sport that contained a ball. I commuted 25 miles each way to work on my bike and most weekends were spent involved in physical activities. When I began to lose the use of my right side, I knew that my days as an outdoor instructor (as I had known it) were over. I couldn't trust myself to belay while climbing and the pace of my walk made wilderness leadership unattractive, and, frankly, dangerous. Faced with these new realities I was forced to carefully evaluate my options and make a few life changing decisions.

At this point in a movie about a person with a disability boldly affirming a new direction, the music begins to soar and there are closeups of a determined face followed by smiling family and friends supporting and cheering the person on. In my experience, life didn't actually conform to the norms of a Hollywood script. Although I have received endless support and encouragement from Barbara, my wife of almost 50 years, my family, and friends and countless demonstrations of kindness and thoughtfulness from total strangers, in general, life just evolved in a positive direction.

I have asked myself many times why the loss of so much of my physical ability never really sent me into periods of anger, depression, or undue frustration. I've concluded that my experiences in outdoor settings and sports in general helped set me up for acceptance and, dare I say it, the joy of the challenge. As a personal mantra I carry the words of my dear friend Bill Affolter, MD: "When you can't get out of it . . . get into it!" How often have those of us involved in outdoor experiential education found this simple statement to be true as we celebrate the conclusion of an adventure that didn't go exactly as planned but nonetheless produced a life changing experience for ourselves and our participants. We reframe the experience and find ways to integrate the challenge into the overall activity. This reframing has become so common and routine for most experienced outdoor leaders that we may not even recognize it in ourselves or others. We, outdoor experiential education practitioners, as a general rule, simply accept what is occurring and work with it as an integral part of the broader experience.

Simple, isn't it? Accept the difficulties one faces and embrace the challenges they afford us. Well, of course, it's not that simple in real life. In my experience, one's ability to flourish during adversity is a function of both personal style and life circumstances. My ability to have the life I'm having and embrace challenge is very much a function of my privilege. If we used an analogy of battery power rather than personal power, my battery was fully charged and has remained charged partly because of a lifetime of mini and maxi events and circumstances that helped position me to accept my situation. In countless ways I was given and maintained the battery power necessary to "get into things" rather than be crushed by them. I've carried the burden of a physical difficulty, but in almost every other way my privilege has protected me from the injustice that can exist for those navigating the world with a disability.

As a leader and teacher and more generally an observer of the human condition, I've found that there is a direct correlation between the amount of energy needed to simply navigate our lives and the ability of people to accept and meet the challenges of life. Anything and everything that drains our battery reduces the likelihood of our dealing with challenges and excelling during the difficult periods of life. I submit that injustice in all its forms is the biggest drain of energy possible and it saps the capacity of people in subtle ways so that when the inevitable and persistent challenges of life arrive, one isn't trying to get into the experience, one's simply trying to get through the experience.

Everything I've written may seem obvious and, in my mind, uncontroversial. Simply stated, the fight for a more just world is critical because it's **justice** that allows us to maintain the energy needed to make the most of our lives.

As a final thought, I am struck by the ways Dr. Nina Roberts maintained her joy, enthusiasm, and optimism while being a leader in our field focused on issues of justice. Nina understood the need to address issues of equity, inclusion, and social justice seriously. She dedicated her life to these issues. However, it's also true that Nina knew that living in the world of the furrowed brow of criticism and critique was unsustainable. Nina taught us that if you attempt to make everything serious, it means that nothing will ever be truly serious. As E. B. White once pondered, "I arise in the morning torn between a desire to improve (or save) the world and a desire to enjoy (or savor) the world. This makes it hard to plan the day." Nina helped teach us how to have wonderful days by doing both changing and savoring. Nina influenced me and changed me, and

I hold her up as the embodiment of a person who showed us how to live with purpose while still enjoying her life.

References

Shenker, I. (1969/7/11). E. B. White: Notes and Comment by Author. *New York Times*, *37*. https://archive.nytimes.com/www.nytimes.com/books/97/08/03/lifetimes/white-notes.html

Photo courtesy of Marcy Marchello, All Out Adventures

Experiential Education and the Aha Moment

Binky Martin-Tollette

My first Association for Experiential Education (AEE) experience was in 1990 in St. Paul, MN. I was aware of the organization through my boss (and future husband), Sanford Tollette, who had previously had one of those "I've found my people moments" during an AEE conference. I've heard many AEE regulars express similar thoughts on finding their people or tribe through AEE. I'm not sure if I really felt that way, but I liked the people I met and resonated with the thinking of most.

One of the most profound experiences I had at that AEE conference was during Bill Proudman's workshop when he led the activity The Crossing. As participants, we lined up on one side of the room. Every time Bill made a statement, we were to decide individually if it applied to our own life. If it did, we were to walk to the other side, notice who was with us on that side and who was not. The questions were light at first and got progressively deeper: "If you have a college degree, step to the other side" or "Step to the other side if you are gay or know someone close to you who is gay" or "If you have lost someone you loved, step to the other side."

During the conference, I met a woman I had trouble relating to for some reason. She happened to be in the workshop, and I noticed that almost every time that she crossed to the other side, I had stayed put, and when I crossed to the other side, she had stayed in her spot. Two White women of similar age seemed to have had almost complete opposite life experiences. I'm still not sure if it was a good idea, but in the debrief I talked about that experience without naming the person. Later, I decided to let her know that she was the person I was talking about. I let her know that the experience helped me recognize that my hesitancy around her simply amounted to differences in life experiences and that I saw it as an opportunity to get to know her and others better.

The last statement that Bill said to the workshop participants was "Step to the other side if you were ever a child." Since most of the statements had been fairly serious, everyone laughed at this statement and crossed to the other side except for two—another woman and me. I was rooted and couldn't move. Of course, I had been a child, and I had come from a very loving home. But as a child of alcoholics, I was always an adult and not a child even though I was a very playful person. That one brief experience during a workshop was an Aha moment, allowing me to see the deep effect my parents' alcoholism had rendered despite the smile and laughter I had used for years to cover the pain—experiential learning to be sure.

In the workplace, being the boss has never been important to me. Making the program work, building relationships, and putting my whole self into the logistics are what drive me. Yet, in 2007, when Little Rock hosted the AEE International Conference, I wanted to be the convenor and being the boss became important. With Sanford and others in our region, I had hosted several regional conferences and had attended many AEE International Conferences. Galvanizing our small host committee to pull off an amazing conference was an AEE high point for me. We were very intentional on diversity and inclusion. The icing on the cake was having Dr. Nina Roberts deliver the Kurt Hahn Address (now The Marina Ewald & Kurt Hahn address), Dr. Jasper Hunt as one keynote, and Minnijean Brown Trickey, one of the Little Rock Nine students who integrated Central High School in 1957, as the other keynote.

I remember thinking one day as the convener that this must be what a man feels like most of the time. I was steady, in control, managing people, and making decisions with ease and without a lot of second guessing. But something else was happening. My body was making some subtle changes. Two months after the conference, the changes were not so subtle, and my gynecologist let me know that I had reached that lovely stage of menopause. No wonder I felt like a man—my estrogen had taken a hike! Some might think this diminishes my competency to suggest that low estrogen played a role in my leadership. But I am suggesting just the opposite—I have always been a leader in my own way despite obstacles, including hormonal changes.

Sanford became my husband in 1995. Only a handful of people were aware that we were dating, mostly because we worked together. I remember seriously thinking that we would each go about our own ways, marry other people (within our respective races) and then find each other again when we were senior citizens and people didn't care whether or not the relationship was interracial. I'm so glad I didn't hold onto that thought! Twenty-six years and two daughters later, we have had very few negative racial issues related to our marriage, and I get to spend every day with the love of my life.

Through my husband and children, I have learned so much about racial nuances and still have much to learn. I take my role as ally seriously because lives and livelihood can depend on it. Sometimes my role is to listen. Sometimes I need to shine the light that a rude White person may be just rude to everyone and not just People of Color. Sometimes I choose to open the discussion.

At a recent camp breakfast, a visitor and donor to the camp made the comment to the campers and staff that it makes her blood boil when she sees an athlete take a knee. I cringed and knew we needed to have a conversation about this. No one confronted this elderly woman because they were too respectful. No one talked to Sanford or me about it, but I knew they needed to process it, so we opened the conversation in a staff meeting. They vented their sadness and frustration that the visitors did not understand the symbolism of athletes kneeling during the national anthem. Respecting their opinions, we asked for their recommendations regarding future interactions with visitors on political matters. Sanford and I took their suggestions and shared it with the visitors. The visitors listened to the staff concerns and out of respect agreed to not offer words of wisdom about politically charged topics in the future.

I'm so ready for the world to embrace differences for what they are and not for something bigger that manifests as a barrier. AEE members may not get it right all the time, but I have always appreciated the platform AEE provides people regardless of any "isms" to learn experientially about themselves and those around or beyond them. AEE allows people to acknowledge the fear, move it out of the way (even if only for a while), and dive into the realm of possibilities.

Photo courtesy of Robbie Francis

Understanding Justice, Equity, Diversity, and Inclusion as a Young Person of Color

Sarita Gray

I am fortunate enough to say I never felt alone in this journey understanding justice, equity, diversity, and inclusion (JEDI) as a Person of Color. With all the mentors I've had, each one said the same thing in their own words—don't let them silence you. As I grow and accept the fact that I will not have the same privileges as others, this advice has stuck with me. I think this quotation displayed in the Holocaust Memorial Museum frames it well.

> First they came for the Socialists, and I did not speak out— Because I was not a Socialist. Then they came for the Trade Unionists, and I did not speak out—Because I was not a Trade Unionist. Then they came for the Jews, and I did not speak out— Because I was not a Jew. Then they came for me—and there was no one left to speak for me. (Martin Niemöller, 2022)

Thanks to my family and upbringing, I've been involved in the outdoor education world. This has afforded me the honor of knowing many amazing people as well as showed me how rare these people are. I now work for Sonoma County Regional Parks. I'm proud of myself for making it through the process of getting this job. The preparations for the interview and the on-the-job training left me in tears each day as I battled with the question of whether I could do it. I would later learn that I could and also became aware of the feeling of being out of place somehow.

Later, as I sat in a circle with my coworkers at our inservice training, I realized the drastic lack of diversity representation. How could the work I do for the public have only one representative of someone who looks like me? Being an advocate for People of Color (POC), how did I not see this right away? It was like growing up all over again and trying to find a Barbie doll who looked like me but never coming even close. It made me reconsider how the children in the public we work with view us as public servants. I wondered if they only see me as a token diversity staff person and that makes me feel sad.

I am aware of the ongoing mission to bring more diversity into the outdoors but had never been in a situation where I had first-hand understanding of this mountain of a challenge. Being a young POC, I know I need to work harder than others to have my voice heard.

Although I love my job, it comes with challenges. During my first week of staff training, I came up with an idea during an exercise for an issue that we had been struggling with for some time. However, no one listened to me. Then moments later, one of my male coworkers repeated what I had just said only louder and got praised for it. I felt unacknowledged. Another key moment that made me rethink my work environment was when I met one of our reserve lifeguards who had a visible ethnic background. The moment I saw her I remember "fangirling" over her as if she were a superhero. She looked like one, had the presence of one, and made me feel empowered by reminding me I could be just like her.

These incidents are related in the way they both made me feel. The first one made me feel unacknowledged, feeling no one was listening to me. The second experience was uplifting and made me feel that I could do anything and that I was smart enough, too.

These experiences empowered me to reach out to my superiors and express my concerns in an email:

> When we were in our inservice training, there was a lack of diversity awareness and practice of inclusion. I feel it's important since you said we represent the county, and the public watches us. Our inservice training group of 15 only

included two people of color. Although I understand there are many different types of ethnicities, identities, and cultures, I feel it's a concern that there is such little diversity representing the Sonoma County Parks in staffing the lifeguard program.

After reaching out, I was able to communicate my concerns and seek help for a solution. The County administration is aware of these statistics and is currently working to integrate new programs that are targeted specifically for POC communities.

As for my own efforts, I have been helping with one of our swimming programs, educating Spanish-speaking and low-income community members in our area and teaching them about water safety and about available programs and resources. This program is called Vamos A Nadar, and I have thoroughly enjoyed being a part of each session and helping participants.

I would like to credit my motivation and encouragement to Dr. Nina Roberts, who sadly passed away only two days before my inservice training experiences. Knowing someone like Nina for my whole life I've learned quite a few things. For example, Nina announced her ideas and thoughts to the world fearlessly despite the backlash that might occur—never backing down. She has done so much for POC communities. JEDI outdoor work is only made possible by people like her and others who continue to challenge the status quo and fight for those who have been silenced. As I continue in my work now, it's people like Nina who remind me of the big impact this type of work has on people's lives.

My life will be forever changed growing up around women outdoor educators. With each new experience, I carry these empowering women with me by continuing the work they've done. The outdoors has saved my life more times than I can remember, and these experiences have helped me see possibilities. Even in outdoor education work there are challenges that are inevitable. Although I know this, witnessing people who are in this work make decisions for the wrong reasons has left me broken time after time. No person or place will ever be perfect, but our stories are real. In the end, the stories we have lived and shared will be what pushes change for us all. My hope is that we can come together and pay respect to each other's stories and truths and find ways to protect and share them, so they are never forgotten and are passed on to future generations. One person can advocate for change; however, with an entire community's support, not only change but also understanding, healing, and even better solutions are possible.

References

Niemöller M. (2022. July 2) First they came for the socialists. https://encyclopedia.ushmm.org/content/en/article/martin-niemoeller-first-they-came-for-the-socialists

Photo courtesy of Sarita Gray

Honoring Women's Voices

Michael Gass

During my professional career, I have offered over 400 peer reviewed presentations at professional conferences identifying as a cisgender White man. Such presentations are a key part to every academician's development as well as one of the primary vehicles to further the field. While my current presentations remain important, the learnings from my very first presentation have been critical in my professional development. This presentation was a panel discussion with three other professionals. One of the three presenters was Dr. Betty van der Smissen.

I had never met Betty in person, but I had heard her described by others as "strict, demanding, hardworking, and committed to her students." She had numerous publications in legal liability and outdoor activities to her credit. At the end of the presentation, I was feeling quite proud of myself and eager to ask her opinions of my work. I turned to her and asked her in a very proud manner, "Betty, how do you think I did?" In a dry contemplative statement, she said "Young man, that's a good start." Picking my chin up off the floor from my gaping mouth, I muttered some conciliatory responses and faded into the enveloping crowd forming around her.

For the next couple of years, it seemed that every time I did a presentation Betty would attend. She always would wait for others to go ahead and then ask me how I came to my conclusions and what I might consider doing to strengthen my presentation. This was nothing I asked for and I never had been a student at one of Betty's universities where she taught. It was just her belief that she was as one professional investing in another colleague for the betterment of the field.

Two years later I was invited to attend a meeting at the Merrowvista Education Center to organize the development of the first Association for Experiential Education (AEE) Accreditation Standards for Adventure Programming. Betty was there, but so was Molly Hampton from the National Outdoor Leadership School (NOLS) and Priscilla McClung from the Outward Bound National Office. Betty's voice was relentless in fostering a standard that we only settle on producing products of excellence. On more than one occasion she stood strong in asking her 25 colleagues to make sure they were delivering content and process that would meet the standards they wanted to achieve.

A few years later I was fortunate enough to be selected to serve as the first Chair of the Accreditation Council. For me these beginning years were greatly aided by the wisdom and experience of Dr. Rita Yerkes, Reb Gregg, Cathy Hansen-Stamp, and Betty van der Smissen. After Jeff Liddle left three years into my term of office, the council and I further benefited from the selection of Sky Gray as the director of the accreditation program with Bill Zimmerman as her colleague. Sky's efforts brought a great deal of success to the accreditation program due to her insights and collegial approach.

Publications by Drs. Deb Sugerman and Jude Hirsch and the development of AEE accreditation standards for Outdoor Behavior Healthcare (OBH) have solidified the accreditation program as it enters its third decade of operations. I have watched my colleague Dr. Anita Tucker join with Drs. Christine Norton, Maurie Lung, Maddy Liebling, Bobbi Beale, Ellen Behrens, and Joanna Bettmann identify needs, work "the system," craft, educate, join their energies, share their "magic," and advocate for what needs to be challenged. Without the different forms of listening, speaking up, and work by these women, we would not be where we are today. We have been privileged to witness and benefit from the growth of women's influence and voice.

And while Nina Roberts embodied these important characteristics and rich qualities, it is her voice that stood out the most. Whether it was debating a point, supporting the critical changes brought about through diversity, speaking out against social injustices, or serving as a champion against social inequities, her presence was primarily announced through her voice. The only thing that exceeded her voice and its presence was her infectious laughter that could easily be heard in the largest of auditoriums.

Have Betty, Nina, and all the other women in between made a difference? In answering this question, I turn full circle and see more new and emerging women leaders. Representing the emerging generation, Casey Blum is affecting educational change as the cofounder and codirector of the Shenandoah, a one-of-a-kind, 177-foot, square-rigged topsail schooner that conducts weeklong educational programming for middle school students and semester-long college programs. Marli Williams has founded Camp YES, a camp for adult women focusing on play and personal growth. Her program's mission is to inspire and empower women to make positive change in their community and lives. Amaryth Dolcino is the co-owner and director of the Sedona Mountain Bike Academy (SMBA). Besides being recognized as the leading mountain bike coaching program in the southwestern United States, SMBA provides discounted mountain bike programs for area youth, U.S. Forest Service, and other organizations in the community. These three emerging young women mirror the strong voices and actions made by the path of Nina and others. As I think about Betty, Nina, and the women who follow them, we have all benefited from their unyielding and supportive voices of excellence in experiential leadership, programming, and research.

Find the good in people
Choose your attitude
Be compassionate
Walk humbly
Do justice
Be there
Serve

Photo courtesy of the Roberts Family

Justice and Joy

Lara Mendel

"This is what peace looks like," Vicki said, gesturing to the diverse group of one hundred 4th and 5th graders. The 16-year-old youth leader's voice was filled with emotion as she spoke. Of the many magical moments that I've experienced in my three decades working in experiential education, this is one, in particular, that I've been thinking about lately.

The students had just finished a powerful activity at The Mosaic Project's Outdoor School, one that captures the complexity of our world, with all its unfairness, messiness, and joy. They were now discussing how they wanted to create a more just, inclusive, peaceful world. Nine-year-old Jeremiah stood up to say, "I don't even know what peace looks like. In my generation, all we've seen is fighting." And that's when Vicki responded, "This is what peace looks like, people of so many different backgrounds, sharing with, listening to, and empathizing with one another. This, right here, is what peace looks like."

I must admit, I have often struggled to remain hopeful during this challenging, strange time. It is memories like this one that keep me going. They remind me how much each moment of understanding, belonging, fun, and peace that we create as experiential educators matters and how crucial it is to show our young people these other possibilities of what the world can be. If there is going to be a chance of creating more inclusive, just, joyful, and peaceful communities, educators must inspire young people with experiences that help them imagine what such communities might look like. We must also give them the tools to turn their imaginations into reality. Their wisdom can then inspire us to keep creating more magical, empowering moments. Creating these special moments is what Dr. Nina Roberts was all about, and she specialized in infusing them with joy. She recognized that justice work can be intense, challenging, and messy but also that it can strengthen communities and can be fun! At Mosaic, we are working towards educational experiences and communities that are better for everyone. That is a joyful goal! We also want our programs to be microcosms of the world we want to see, a more just and joyful one. If we are to do that, we must bring the justice and also the joy, just as Nina did.

Like Nina, we can bring games, laughter, and music to our students of all ages. We can remind them that while injustice in our world is a reality, so are peace and love. We can recognize and celebrate those moments of deep connection among our students. And we can inspire gratitude for each learning experience we have together. Justice, joy, and gratitude–Nina embodied these qualities so beautifully. I can think of no better way to honor her legacy than by sharing them with our students.

Photo courtesy of Sherry Bagley

A Testimonio of Transformational Justice

Esther Ayers

This is my testimonio—a short narrative toward transformational justice. Testimonios are used as a methodology to call attention to social injustices (The Latina Feminist Group, 2001). After graduating in 2014, I integrated adventure therapy as a treatment method with primarily Latinx clients at a community-based agency, supervised by Gary Stauffer. Thereafter, I obtained full licensure for clinical social work and began a Ph.D. in Chicano/Latino Studies at Michigan State University (MSU) in 2018. I share my testimonio of an incident I endured with the organizers of the Symposium on Experiential Education Research (SEER) to spotlight resources that supported me during this challenging event, including authentic allies. I close this reflection piece with a call to action to bring awareness to transformational justice.

The Incident

In 2020, during my second year of graduate school, my research focused on mental health, Latinx communities, and adventure therapy. I was encouraged to submit an abstract to SEER, part of the Association for Experiential Education (AEE). I was hesitant since my work focused primarily on theory rather than data analysis, but I decided to submit an abstract. My abstract was not accepted. I requested a meeting with a SEER editor to help me understand areas where I could grow as a researcher and writer. Afterwards, a Zoom meeting with the editor occurred that left me with three serious concerns. First, I was told that SEER did not accept theoretical or conceptual papers, which I later found out was not true. Second, the SEER editor had no idea of culturally congruent theories and methods used to advocate for historically underrepresented groups. Third, I inquired about the number of people of color who were editors for SEER. In my investigation, I noticed there was not a Diversity, Equity, and Inclusion statement posted on the website. After the first meeting, the SEER editor's strategy to help strengthen my writing skills was that I rely on my dissertation chair and research peers who had similar interest, including Dr. Christine Norton, Dr. Anita Tucker, and Dr. Nina Roberts.

This SEER incident prompted emails, virtual meetings, and phone consultations. But due to unforeseen circumstances, I chose to focus on my health for a few days. Upon my return, Dr. Norton suggested I work with the SEER editors to resubmit. As advised, I resubmitted, and Dr. Curt Davidson met with me to sharpen my abstract and guide me with the resubmission process. My abstract, "A Literature Review of Adventure Therapy with LatinX Youth in Community-based Settings: Implications for Research and Practice," was accepted by SEER for the 2020 conference.

I continue to ask questions about how this incident could occur in 2020? It seemed surreal that the sense of belonging and positive relationships I established in AEE with adventure therapy researchers and practitioners could result in this convoluted process in another part of the organization. I was surprised that SEER editors were not familiar with critical race theory (CRT) and seemingly did not understand intersectionality and CRT.

During this SEER situation, I experienced microaggressions. Microaggressions are forms of racism that are witnessed and felt in covert ways (Garcia & Johnson Guerrero, 2016). For me, it was this sense of feeling "othered" by the incident, and it made me question if I even belonged in academia.

I reflected on Black, Indigenous, and People of Color (BIPOC) scholars from diverse disciplines that warned me of these types of microaggressions, which have a deep effect on representation in higher education. The National Center for Education Statistics

151

(2020) reports that less than 3% of higher education faculty positions in the United States are held by BIPOC. These statistics, combined with my personal experience, made me wonder how academia shares knowledge about historically underrepresented groups and who decides what knowledge is shared?

Coping Strategies

In spite of the pain of this SEER incident, I was able to grow and learn through the process. The first technique that helped me cope with the experience was reflecting on why education matters. I chose to pursue higher education because I wanted to read and write from an epistemological viewpoint conducive to amplifying voices of color. More specifically, I wanted a perspective that amplified BIPOC communities and their mental health and integrated culturally congruent theories that infused strength-based methods, such as testimonios. In addition to tapping into mi gente, my people, in academia, which entailed more readings across diverse scholars, I used music by Selena Quintanilla to regulate and revive my energy and stamina.

Authentic Allies

Also, I relied on my authentic allies, a diverse group of folx who demonstrated unconditional support through the good, bad, and indifferent parts of this incident. In 2018, I was encouraged to attend SEER. During the SEER presentations, I remember not seeing folx that looked like me, a short, dark brown Latina. Then, in 2019, I attended the Therapeutic Adventure Professional Group (TAPG) Best Practices conference, where I saw some of my authentic allies present as keynote speakers. In 2020, I presented as an AEE Activate speaker on "Community is at the heart of what keeps us together," where I shared how mental health impacted my life and identified my passion for adventure therapy. I used a combination of these observations to shape my understanding and perceptions of the importance of allies and belonging. I leaned on the suggestion offered by the SEER editor to consult with scholars with similar research interests. Now I continue to grow with brave scholars such as Dr. Roberts. I say brave because scholarship and teaching about historically underrepresented groups are forms of activism that challenge mainstream knowledge.

The road to ethnic studies scholarship is lined with roadside graves of drop-outs, even at the professorial level, with early deaths including deaths by suicide and, with psychological and physical ailments related to frustrations, stress, and bouts of defeatism (Perez, 2010, p. 130). I relied on my strong social support network to guide me during this time of adversity, including core scholars and practitioners Dr. Norton, Dr. Tucker, Tony Alvarez, and Gary Stauffer. By collaborating with allies in my academic social network, I obtained access to supportive resources *con mi familia*, *mi comunidad*, and my mentors beyond AEE and sought traditional healings through spirituality, nature, music, and beyond.

In consulting with my mentors, I continued to do what WE do best, as a *comunidad*. I continued to read and write as part of my healing process. I listened to courageous scholars Dr. Norton and Dr. Tucker. *Ellas me dieron animo para seguir adelante*; they gave me courage to move forward. I continued to build my research with diverse interdisciplinary scholars within ethnic studies and adventure therapy that focus research on community-based healthcare agencies. I became critical of literature that focused on communities of color only using a deficit lens.

Building on BIPOC researchers within the *Journal of Experiential Education* (JEE) and AEE, I identified with Dr. Roberts, a brave scholar who inspired me. Her work built on scholars who focused on social justice dating back to the 1970s in the fields that use experiential education. A few articles meaningfully linked with my research because they shed light on the need for cultural representation (Roberts & Drogin, 1993; Roberts & Henderson, 1997; Warren et al., 2014). Another piece of work by Roberts and Spears (2020) succinctly placed an emphasis on affirmative efforts that shed light on the historical roles of African Americans, including Lancelot Jones and Martha Aikens, as visionary leaders in the outdoors. Something about Dr. Roberts' (2021) work that I aspire to model is to reject dichotomous perspectives. She challenged BIPOC researchers to question our own assumptions so we can reflect on our own biases, while at the same time demonstrating the importance of partnering with interdisciplinary scholarship to dismantle inequities. To me, it was a light bulb moment because it was literature about knowing and understanding who is telling the story and the importance of having awareness of historical cultural representation in the outdoors. Dr. Roberts' work made me feel like my passion and writing for social justice was important. My voice mattered, my narrative mattered, and the idea of belonging in AEE was revived and renewed.

Call to Action

As a Latina scholar born and raised in the Midwest, I offer my testimonio of transformative justice by reconstructing the SEER incident. To begin, as I reflect on the SEER incident, I recognize areas of growth on both sides. I am proud that some policies and guidelines have been updated. For example, *The Journal of Experiential Education* published a recommendation for manuscripts with the ultimate goal of updating research reporting standards and guidelines (Seaman et al., 2020). Also, after the SEER incident, I noticed there is a DEI statement on the SEER website. Equally important, in the summer of 2021, I was asked to be an editor for SEER abstracts, which has been a service that has allowed me to reinvent my feelings of belonging within SEER.

It is our duty as a collective to build on those who left us, to continue to join with those who are aligned with us to learn, grow, *y seguir adelante* as a collective community. As Roberts and Spears (2020) eloquently asserted, "The only way we can change the outdoors is by a massive alteration of mindsets, including institutions across varying disciplines, from passively nonracist to actively antiracist. At the end of the day, the sun always sets—and the start of a new dawn sets the sail for either a new beginning or increasing the momentum" (p. 185). Let's follow the sun together and dance. I'm ready to get this party started, are you? *Que descanses en paz,* Dr. Roberts.

References

Garcia, G., Johnson-Guerrero, M.P. (2016). Challenging the utility of racial microaggressions framework through a systematic review of racially biased incidents on campus, *Journal of Critical Scholarship on Higher Education and Student Affairs, 2*(1), Article 4. https://ecommons.luc.edu/jcshesa/vol2/iss1/4

Latina Feminist Group (D. C. de Filippis, D. C., Cuadraz, G. H., Fiol-Matta, L., Flores-Ortiz, Y. G., Quintanales, M. F., Rivero, E., Souza, C., Acevedo, L. del A., Alarcon, N., Saldívar-Hull, C., Behar, R., Benmayor, R., Benmayor, R., & Lomas C. (2001). *Telling to live,* del Alba Acevedo, L., Alarcon, N., Alvarez, C., Behar, R., Benmayor, R., Cantú, N. E., ... & Zavella, P. (Eds.). *Telling to live: Latina feminist testimonios.* Duke University Press. https://doi.org/10.1215/9780822383284

National Center for Education Statistics. (2022). Characteristics of Postsecondary Faculty. Condition of Education. U.S. Department of Education, Institute of Education Sciences. https://nces.ed.gov/programs/coe/indicator/csc

Pérez, L. E. (2010). Enrique Dussel's Etica de la liberación, U.S. Women of color decolonizing practices, and coalitionary politics amidst difference. *Qui Parle: Critical Humanities and Social Sciences, 18*(2), 121–146. https://doi.org/10.5250/quiparle.18.2.121

Roberts, N. S., & Drogin, E. B. (1993). The outdoor recreation experience: Factors affecting participation of African American women. *Journal of*

Experiential Education, *16*(1), 14–18. https://doi.org/
10.1177/105382599301600102

Roberts, N. S., & Henderson, K. A. (1997). Women of color in the outdoors:
Culture and meanings. *Journal of Experiential Education*, *20*(3), 134–
142. https://doi.org/10.1177/105382599702000305

Roberts, N. S., & Spears, A. (2020). Connecting the dots: Why does what
and who came before us matter? *Parks Stewardship Forum*, *36*(2),
173–187. https://doi.org/10.5070/P536248260

Roberts, N. S. (2021). "White Savior" as duly provocative or enforced civility
with unintended consequences? A response to Anderson, Knee, &
Mowatt. *Journal of Leisure Research*, *52*(5), 551–556. https://doi.org/
10.1080/00222216.2020.1854547

Seaman, J., Dettweiler, U., Humberstone, B., Martin, B., Prince, H., & Quay,
J. (2020). Joint recommendations on reporting empirical research in
outdoor, experiential, environmental, and adventure education
journals. *Journal of Experiential Education*, *43*(4), 348–364. https://
doi.org/10.1177/1053825920969443

Warren, K., Roberts, N. S., Breunig, M., & Alvarez, M. A. (Tony) G. (2014).
Social justice in outdoor experiential education: A state of knowledge
review. *Journal of Experiential Education*, *37*(1), 89–103. https://
doi.org/10.1177/1053825913518898

Photo courtesy of AEE

Understanding the Perceptions African Americans Have About the Environment and Nature and How These Perceptions Influence Their Behavior and Environmental Commitment

Tameria M. Warren

My family was part of the "Great Migration" of African Americans who moved to midwestern, eastern, and western states during the early to mid-20th century. Along with that mass movement came a cache of practices, stories, knowledge bases, and experiences connected to outdoor and natural spaces. Many of my kin settled in Southeast Michigan, which was home to the country's "Big Three" automobile manufacturers. Their scheduled shutdowns of production allowed my family and others to return to the south and help their families on their farms or with other manual labor. These routine travels allowed African Americans to retain traditional practices and exposed their children and younger generations to the "old ways" of their southern family members.

My personal summer road trips to Mississippi, mostly every Independence Day weekend, developed in me an appreciation for the ways that African Americans engage with the land. Playing outdoors and witnessing family members hunting, gardening, fishing, and passing along family traditions, planted early seeds of my environmentalism. Subsequently, my urban experiences of inequitable zoning, polluting industries, lax regulations, and burgeoning environmental injustices plaguing communities of color shed a contrasting light on the environment and its connection to African Americans.

My experiences and my desire to explore my personal connections, including familial patterns to the environment to determine if similarities existed with other African Americans became the focus of my doctoral research. My research was guided by the research question: What are the perceptions that African Americans have about the environment and nature, and how do these perceptions influence their behavior and environmental commitment? I looked at ecopsycological elements, historical narratives, and current social dynamics of African American culture to understand their frame of reference in connection to the environment.

African American's juxtaposition between urban living and outdoor recreation was a central focus of my research. I studied the perceptions and behaviors exhibited by African American adults in Michigan (metropolitan Detroit area) and South Carolina (metropolitan Columbia area). Many of the participants in both groups were African Americans with environmentally-related careers or worked in spaces where environmental and sustainability issues were regularly discussed. The geographic locations accounted for my family's places of residency as well as the pattern of midwestern and southern experiences that shaped my connection to the environment.

My research relied on methodologies that drew from the experiences of the participants and myself as the researcher. Using ethnography, autoethnography, phenomenology, narrative inquiry research methods, and critical race theory, I created a research study that used interview sessions and questionnaires to generate qualitative and quantitative data.

I gathered data on the African American participants:

♦ Outdoor childhood activities

♦ Adult involvement in the participants' youth-related outdoor experiences

♦ Concerns about the environment

- Experiences with negative impacts on the environment

- Perceptions of individuals and mainstream organizations associated with the environmental movement and their interactions with African American communities

- Current and potential environmental behaviors

- Outdoor activities that People of Color (POC) selected

- Factors contributing to the participants' environmental actions and decisions

Seven major themes emerged from the participants' responses:

- Early Influence

- Connection to the Environment/Nature

- Perceptions

- Behaviors/Activities

- Environmental Concerns

- Cultural Factors

- Awareness

Participants expressed an understanding that environmental issues were prevalent within their communities, with multiple responses describing cultural and racial differences pertaining to environmentalists. For example, the consolidation of their answers given for an interview question regarding stereotypes typically associated with environmentalists referred to characteristics often assigned to White Americans within a specific economic category. Their most frequently used words to describe environmentalists included "White," "Caucasian," "tree hugger," "middle class," "educated," and "hippies." Most of the participants engaged in the ordinary tasks that would be recognized as an environmental action, such as recycling and repurposing household items. Unanimous responses indicated that participants had engaged in some form of outdoor activity during childhood and most expressed that time spent outdoors or in nature is a positive experience.

There was recognition that the environment plays an integral part in the lives of African Americans. Many of the experiences from their childhood and adult years pertained to agricultural activities (such as gardening and farming) and fishing that occurred on both public lands and properties owned by their families. Additionally, participants acknowledged that as children they rarely discussed the environment and nature including conservation, preservation, and pollution prevention measures with their parents or other children or adults. What they did experience, however, was language through demonstration. Specific actions about managing or taking care of the earth were learned through hands-on approaches rather than verbal communication.

Lastly, participants in this study overwhelmingly cited Whites and elements often associated with Whites as the frame of reference for environmentalism. However, African Americans are just as interested in and concerned about the environment yet may not perceive themselves as environmentalists. For example, an interesting occurrence that happened during multiple interview sessions was a perceived realization by some participants that they could be classified as environmentalists given the responses they provided. While most participants expressed an understanding of their significance within the environment, others discussed how the conversations during the interviews enlightened their perspectives.

In addition to the interview sessions, the participants in both groups completed and submitted questionnaires that further inquired about their connection to the environment. The study results indicate that there are significant correlations between some environmental and social aspects exhibited by the participants, specifically the association of childhood outdoor activities and adult involvement for the Michigan group and correlation between childhood outdoor activities and relationship with nature (and, in turn, that relationship and a concern for the environment) for the South Carolina group. Moreover, one test showed an association between concern for the environment and frequency in doing environmental activities for the Michigan group. Overall, these African Americans are interested in the environment and some of the components associated with it.

I identified the following conclusions from my research:

- The importance of exposure to nature and outdoor activities during the formative years of a person's life and how that involvement can help shape one's perspective about the environment.

- Factors that affect African Americans' engagement in environmental activities include internal perceptions, stereotypes, environmental justice measures, and other components.

- African Americans' increased participation in nature and outdoor activities is promising.

I use my research results to inform individuals, especially those within the Black community, that African Americans are not outliers within the environmental movement and our connection to the environment is in tandem with our history and present journey throughout the African diaspora. I encourage others to use this research as a tool for dismantling perceptions about African Americans and the environment and once laid bare, use it to facilitate dialogue and generate more narratives about the Black environmental experience. Having the opportunity to engage other African Americans in conversations about the environment reinforced my desire to reshape the ways that society sees and discusses environmental issues. But more importantly, it reaffirmed that I am not alone in a green space that is seemingly "White." Connections to the environment are decidedly more diverse and expansive than often projected, and this research, specifically the interactions with participants, magnified the presence and significance of POC in the environmental arena.

References

Warren, T. M. (2016). Understanding the Perceptions African Americans have about the Environment and Nature and how those Perceptions Influence Their Behavior and Environmental Commitment. (Publication No. 10142442) [doctoral dissertation Prescott College]. ProQuest Dissertations Publishing.

Photo courtesy of Robbie Francis

Towards Global Inclusion and Belonging

Stuart Slay

I worked at an international school in South Korea for nearly ten years. Raised in the United States and identifying as a White cisgender man at this stage of my life, this time represents over half of my working career. Our mission in South Korea was to build a school-based outdoor education program modeled after a sister school and program in Southern California.

What started for me as a curious adventure evolved into an eye-opening and life shaping journey. During the first several years, I was fascinated by the foods and how the groups of children respectfully shared family-style lunches on a tarp without evidence of food stress or bullying. As American instructors, the English-only policy bothered us, but we couldn't articulate why. There was a clear need in the school and program to speak the same language, but the policy felt insensitive.

The staff grew the program's course offerings year by year by exploring a small, densely-populated, and long-historied countryside and culture. As each year went by, I began to find myself peering deeper into the cultural iceberg, discovering deeper cultural norms and values hidden below the surface. If there was one, singular moment that illuminated and articulated the deepest layers of the iceberg, it was during a meeting with a new acquaintance whom I was aiming to build a relationship with to gain access to a new, long sought-after paddle and backpacking course area.

He was a man of small stature but great personality and enthusiasm. He dressed like a Buddhist monk but kept a stack of empty soju liquor bottles to greet you as you entered his front yard. According to my colleagues who translated for me, he swore like a sailor and spoke in an "old-timey" way. He grew gochu peppers and picked mushrooms. As a younger man, he nearly completed a PhD but decided the university hoops weren't worth the trouble. He smoked like a chimney. He referred to himself as "Neung-ha," a pen name he signed to his artful and expressive calligraphy, which I keep framed on my wall.

As the town elder, Neung-ha held much respect within the small village of Wit-du-sil, a tiny mountain village of about 30 farmers. During the Japanese occupation in the early 19th century, these mountains provided refuge for the Korean partisans as they raided Japanese supply and transportation lines. Centuries earlier kings and noblemen fled to these hills to rule in exile. Today, the local villagers complain about the provincial park as a refuge for boars, who invade their lands and destroy their crops. In a few villages further down the road, we met a woman who told us about the war between the north and the south, some 70 years ago. She remembers seeing American soldiers but didn't realize there was a civil war where the Americans backed the South until years after it was over. In my history books growing up, the Korean war was sometimes referred to as "the forgotten war," if mentioned at all.

I sat on this man's floor cross legged for hours. My knees and butt hurt and I wiggled with discomfort. Cho, my good friend who worked as our logistics manager, patiently sat stiff and upright as she translated from my quick and rambling American filled jargon through her Kiwi English to her native Seoul Korean and back again from an elder, academic yet quip Korean. This man, I knew, held the keys to these lands. I had been on a years-long journey to find the perfect course area to support the program's curriculum, an area that could accommodate many students with similar group itineraries. The area we sought required age and skill-level appropriate backpacking and paddling within scenic and ancient Korea. I was ready to engage him in every way possible to gain his voice of support for our future courses here, including entertaining his life story, drinking and eating as friends, and discussing the merits of experiential education philosophy and methodology for the youth of Korea.

He said, "You're a neocolonist with your experiential education ideas." His words cut straight through me as I stared forward to the ground. Cho paused to recollect and continue the translation: "If what you are describing is experiential education, it was here long before you. The version you describe originally came to us from the Japanese, although even then it was here centuries before they were."

I sat, patiently and painstakingly listening as my knees ached and back slouched. I stretched my legs out to give them a break as the message and its stinging intent passed around the room to my awaiting English-only ears. An uncomfortable silence between the three of us split the room. "Go on, tell him," I imagined him thinking.

"….he says to sit up straight, and how dare you come into his room to slouch and stretch like a lazy *waeguk* [foreigner]…" I quickly recoiled and straightened up, but felt a low, deep embarrassment at my offense.

He said, that is experiential education in Korea. You do, the teacher corrects, and the student reflects. What it means to be, to be yourself, and to be yourself in the presence of elders is different between the west and the east. By stretching out you aim to comfort yourself. But to us, your stretching is loud, lazy, and selfish. I don't fault you for being or doing normal in your country, but you should show cognizance of what is 'normal' here.

I sat tall but felt small. My inner shame bore outward. "The reflection is supposed to hurt," he said. "That's where the learning

165

comes from. By coming here to claim you are 'bringing' experiential education to us, you are merely perpetuating the colonial tendencies and habits of mind our Japanese colonizers brought."

He stood up and picked an encyclopedic-sized book off his shelf. He studied it for a minute, found his page, then shoved it toward Cho.

"Here," he said, "Take this home with you and study it. This is an article describing just that journey. You study it and translate it for him." The book was a series of articles in Korean, Japanese, and Chinese compiled by a monk.

I reflect on this day often. What were we doing here? What purpose were we fulfilling by building a California version of outdoor education on the other side of the world? What assumptions did I bring to this program that, if revealed to me, I would come to associate with deep shame and embarrassment?

As experiential educators move forward in today's global society, let's be cognizant of what we bring and what we claim as truth and "good." Neung-ha enthusiastically supported our program and was key to us keeping our access when the local government changed. After the first program there, the villagers exclaimed how they felt joy at the sound of youth in the village after a nearly 30-year hiatus.

We can recognize the benefits of experiential and outdoor programming as we further our missions in today's contemporary and global society. However, we should also open ourselves to the influences of the past that got us here, including the history, traditions, values, and methods of the local people and places where we work.

We can learn and be cognizant of what we bring when we claim the power and "good" that experiential education can do. Including the local people and their histories in our experiential education, philosophy, and goals serve our participants in finding relevance and meaning from their experiences. In turn, we can grow on a parallel path. Identifying and incorporating these local histories strengthen and make the programs and goals more relevant to students and local communities.

Photo courtesy of Denise Mitten

Travel with Purpose: International Service-Learning in Costa Rica

Pavlína Látková

During the past three years, humanity found itself at one of the lowest points of its history. The concurrent experiences of increased levels of racial and ethnic prejudice and related hate crimes, the long-lasting global pandemic, accelerating climate change, and yet another economic crisis further exacerbated by the war in Ukraine have arguably resulted in our communities being divided and people's actions being powered by fear. What we need is more compassion and respect for one another to build equitable communities.

More than ever, there is an urgency for educators to teach for social justice within the classroom setting. Yet, the preparedness of educators varies when it comes to creating meaningful educational social justice opportunities in the classroom.

Experiential learning could be a dynamic methodology in an educator's toolbox. Using this methodology can help educators transfer their social justice knowledge into enabling students to learn skills applicable to real-life scenarios. Students need to acquire these skills to lead our communities into the future, where opinions may differ, yet hearts can be united for the greater good of humanity.

Personally, I value experiential learning for its hidden power to build a sense of community in and outside the classroom. It reliably increases when experiential learning integrates community service projects that provide students with opportunities to identify and solve real problems in communities. The research has demonstrated that participating in service learning and reflecting on one's experiences teaches students life skills and provides positive outcomes such as acceptance of diversity, civic responsibility, democratic citizenship, and community engagement (Brandell & Hinck, 1997; Howard, Markus, & King, 1993; Shumer & Belbas, 1996; Strage, 2000).

The addition of international travel can also increase global awareness and civic-mindedness and build intercultural understanding (Crabtree, 2008). My personal travel experiences enabled me to explore the world beyond the content of textbooks, beyond national boundaries, and beyond my wild imagination. My personal transformation facilitated by international service learning inspired me, a university professor, to design an international service-learning course in hopes my students too will undergo a personal transformation while expanding their horizons beyond the "San Francisco Bay Area bubble" and experiencing realities other than their own.

San Francisco State University's (SF State) RPT 470 Travel with Purpose: Costa Rica is an elective 11-week course consisting of traditional classroom experience. Students conduct research and share their knowledge about Costa Rica's history, culture, geography, politics, and economy. They facilitate team-building activities to learn about one another and to practice leading activities in English and Spanish in preparation for school service projects. In addition, outside classroom experiential and service-learning experiences are used. Students organize a fundraiser and collect donations for school and recreational supplies before the trip. After the trip, the class sessions focus on posttrip debriefing, reflections, and learning about students' individual experiences by watching students' videos featuring their trip highlights.

In Costa Rica, students participate in approximately 40 hours of service-learning experience that includes lectures and workshops, facilitation of recreation activities, and cultural immersion in less crowded Afro-Caribbean communities of Limon, Tortuguero, and Cahuita as well as the Yorkín Indigenous community. These areas of the Costa Rican Caribbean coast, not frequented by Western visitors, seem to be "forgotten" by the Costa Rican government and mainstream society.

Specifically, students participate in two natural resources conservation projects and two community-based development projects during their visit to Costa Rica. The ARA Manzanillo nonprofit project focuses on the Scarlet and Great Green macaws rescue and reintroduction into the wild. The students assist with daily tasks supporting the ARA Manzanillo project's mission.

The Stibrawpa community rural ecotourism project aims to share and preserve the Bribri community. As part of the project, students plant trees and perform basic trail maintenance. During the Tortuguero and the Yorkín elementary schools and kindergarten school visits, students engage with youth by leading recreational activities and games. They also distribute school and recreational supplies collected through their fundraising efforts in the San Francisco Bay Area.

The service-learning experience is never the same, yet always rewarding to facilitate. Students approach the unknown with open minds and hearts. The class gives them a platform to search for answers, discover and learn, connect, share their fears of the unknown, and build trust and a sense of community (within the classroom setting and communities visited during the trip). Ultimately, this form of experiential learning provided them with an opportunity to be themselves and care for one another while giving back to the community.

Pretrip interviews and students' journal reflections confirm that natural beauty, media-portrayed Costa Rica's Pura Vida (Costa Ricans' relaxed attitude towards life, as portrayed by the media), and the opportunity to engage with and help local communities are their main class enrollment and international travel motivators. Students expect to explore the pristine natural beauty—they are excited to see sloths and monkeys and to experience the breathtaking marine life while snorkeling in the Caribbean Sea. They expect to help the local communities by participating in community projects and by delivering school and recreational supplies they collected in the Bay Area.

What students do not anticipate experiencing is an authentic culture and people, 4,000+ years of environmental stewardship practice, and a strong sense of community and pride among the members of marginalized Afro-Caribbean and Indigenous BriBri communities. They also do not expect to develop strong bonds with one another, a sense of belonging and community, and friendships that last beyond college years.

Students in this course typically do not come from privileged families; they are not the traditional U.S. student. These students represent different racial and ethnic groups. Many are first-generation students, often members of low-income and/or marginalized minorities. They are compassionate, resilient, and more mature than one would expect them to be at their age. Yet, they are surprised to learn how privileged and empowered they are in comparison to people they meet during our journey, simply because of their access to resources (e.g., education and related resources, potable water, sanitation, internet, and medical and social services). These resources are not readily available to marginalized populations in Costa Rica. The people they meet display a high level of community resilience against historical oppression.

Course students do not expect to hear heartbreaking stories shared by strong women community leaders and mothers who witnessed first-hand the raw reality of the negative impacts of tourism, such as Western tourists introducing drugs into their communities, causing teenagers to drop out of school and be lured into prostitution. SF State students do not expect to learn about the climate change impacts (and limited government support to offset climate change impacts) affecting the livelihoods and causing family disruption in the BriBri community, who have lived and cared for their lands for thousands of years.

To sustain the BriBri community, the Stibrawpa Association (originally, a group of craftswomen who started to manufacture and sell their handicrafts to tourists) introduced an ecotourism project in the late 1990s. Since its introduction, the ecotourism project has helped diversify the BriBri economy, revitalize their culture undermined by the emigration of their community members, and preserve their forest—their home of 4,000 years. The BriBri ecotourism experience includes lectures and tours highlighting BriBri culture, religion, and traditions as well as lodging and opportunities to purchase handicrafts made by locals.

The 10-day service-learning experience is eye-opening, mind-stimulating, and life-changing. Yet, when students reflect on their experiences upon return to the United States, they realize that when they were learning about and helping marginalized communities, they were also learning about themselves. They were helping themselves undergo a personal transformation into more courageous and compassionate people empowered to become more active members in their communities.

Understanding that no matter how different we are, our hopes and dreams connect us locally and globally. They propel us through the process of exploring, sharing, and embracing our fears and biases. Perhaps, this is the first step to celebrating our differences. In my humble opinion, experiential learning that includes service-learning projects is the most powerful methodology in a teacher's toolbox, because it has the potential to rejuvenate human hearts, and ultimately to help us work together to build more equitable communities locally and globally.

References

Brandell, M. E., & Hinck, S. (1997). Service learning: Connecting citizenship with the classroom. *Civic Engagement*, *30*, 49–56. http://digitalcommons.unomaha.edu/slceciviceng/30

Crabtree, R. D. (2008). Theoretical foundations for international service-learning. *Michigan Journal of Community Service Learning*, *15*(1), 18–36. http://hdl.handle.net/2027/spo.3239521.0015.102

Howard, J. P., Markus, G. B., & King, D. C. (1993). Integrating community service and classroom instruction enhances learning: Results from an experiment. *Educational Evaluation and Policy Analysis*, *15*(4), 410–419. https://www.hks.harvard.edu/fs/dking/service.pdf

Shumer, R., & Belbas, B. (1996). What we know about service learning. *Education and Urban Society*, *28*(2), 208–223. https://eric.ed.gov/?id=EJ522433

Strage, A. A. (2000). Service-learning: Enhancing student learning outcomes in a college-level lecture course. *Michigan Journal of Community Service Learning*, *7*, 5–13.

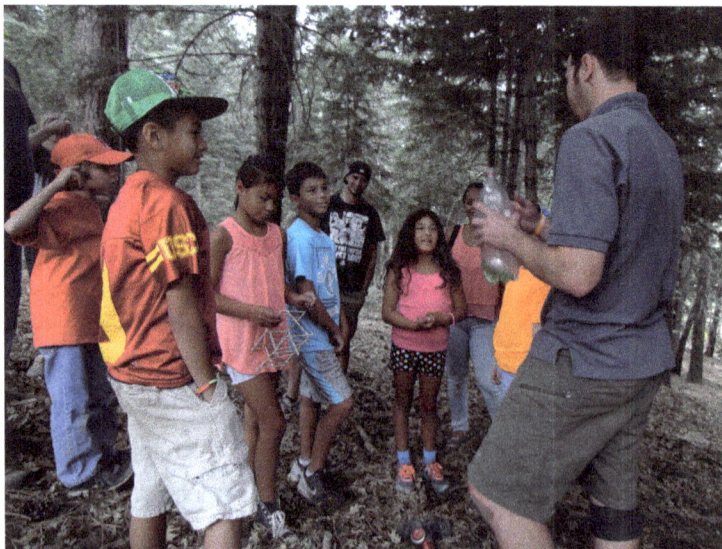

Photo courtesy of AEE

Stay Humble and Stay Curious

Aiko Yoshino

Things that don't kill you, make you stronger: This affirmation of resilience by Friedrich Nietzsche, the German philosopher, remains a conceptual foundation of adventure education and its goal of character development. Yet, I challenge the reader to turn the notion around and critically contemplate the pitfalls of the concept. Resilience brings inner strength yet has a limited ability to eliminate structural inequalities of power.

An Armadillo

Growing up in a homogenous, patriarchal, collectivistic culture like Japan and then moving to the United States created a series of hardships that required growing layers of dynamic protection from my youth through middle-aged adulthood. I was raised in a family with four siblings. A family of such size was and continues to be very rare in Japan, the country with the lowest fertility rate in the world (average of 1.30 children per woman in 2022). My ambitious breadwinner father and caring and frugal mother often argued over how money should be spent to support their family of seven people. The parsimonious lifestyle I developed in my early career enabled me to save enough money to embark for study abroad at Indiana University in the United States, my first choice in graduate programs. Through a mix of hard work and a thick skin, I earned master's and doctoral degrees with a focus in outdoor education.

Studying outdoor education in a place that was reputed to be "a half century ahead" of my country was a dream; however, it also required many sacrifices. Leaving the only language that I had fluently spoken and the known cultural norms of my home country were challenging. These challenges were magnified by the xenophobia I experienced as both individual and serial macro- and microaggressions. Moving far away from the support of my friends and families for multiple years meant that I did not have a social safety net as I walked down the uncertain path to achieve my dream. It was essential for me to develop an armadillo's resilient armor.

Invisible Challenges

In my first few years in the United States, my English comprehension was so limited that I could barely communicate at the level of a 3-year-old. Becoming fluent in English was a necessary obstacle I needed to overcome to reach my ultimate goal. The invisible challenge was my sense of isolation in an unfamiliar environment. Everything was foreign including the food, people, culture, weather, geographical elements, what funny or polite means, and so forth. In retrospect, I lost nearly everything that I had. No job, no financial stability, no mental and physical support from family, no language to communicate with, no friends to talk to, no pride to hold on to, and no home to relax in.

Every step was a series of mistakes and learning. For instance, I ordered my comfort food "rice" but got teased because I was apparently ordering "lice"; I tried to defend myself to a police officer when he pulled me over at an intersection and I said "I crossed on the 'blue' light" (believe me people in Japan say "blue" light instead of "green"); and I've mistakenly bought a bottle of lotion multiple times instead of hair conditioner. My first bite of the classic North American sweets, brownies, ended with unmanageable coughs and watery eyes just like eating wasabi, the green condiment paste that comes with sushi.

Coming out of my first full-time job in Japan as a public-school teacher, I had a false sense of entitlement that I was a decent capable young adult, yet the reality in the United States was harsh. All I had was ego and the thought that I could not back out of this study abroad not only because I left my people and my country to selfishly chase my own dream but also, it'd have proved that I failed to pursue my dream.

A Leaping Frog

As a petite foreign Asian woman, I worked very hard to not allow my smaller stature limit my performance in outdoor field positions where I often worked with taller and stronger co-instructors. This relative physical weakness meant that I needed to take more steps to go the same distance and carry a higher percentage of my body weight. My ability to ask coworkers to slow down or take a larger share of the weight was challenged by my need to prove myself. My peers and advisors often asked some version of "Why did you come to the United States?" My answer was consistently, "To study and to become a better outdoor educator, so that I can build an outdoor education school in Japan." That was the goal that drove me to pursue rock climbing guiding certificates, a wilderness educator certificate, and Wilderness First Responder in a language that was a consistent challenge, a foreign culture that challenged my ability to understand the social context, and immigration laws that constrained my ability to earn enough money to keep myself afloat. I made all of these sacrifices with the hope of being the frog that leapt out of their tiny muddy pond.

A Poisonous Caterpillar

I started my experience like a poisonous caterpillar complete with barbed stinging hairs bristling from all parts of me ready to defend myself against potential social predators. My nerves were on edge attempting to overcome my limited English ability and lack of cultural knowledge to sense if others were harshly judging me. Other people's reactions mattered immensely to me. Are they chuckling at me or with me? Is the joke for pure entertainment or sarcasm that was targeting me? Is that little look judging me or offering support? I intensely studied each move, each reaction, and each facial expression for potential signs of the social rejection I feared.

In the Midwest where I was studying, being the only Asian woman was a common experience for me. Eventually, I decided that the challenges of being constantly vigilant were not supporting my goals of working with and learning from my students and coworkers. I emerged from this period of self-reflection with fewer barbs but a thicker skin. I decided I didn't have to be so sensitive about the mistakes I made or feel embarrassed about my social faux pas. I shed my needles and decided to be more vulnerable. I worried less about those who might be judging me or microaggressions and opened myself to learning more and developing relationships that mattered.

A Weed

Persistence and tears paid off. I was like a little weed coming out of a crack in the asphalt. My money problems abated when I landed my first job as a cleaning lady, then a camp counselor, and then a trip leader. This led to opportunities to become a supervisor and program director.

When I led outdoor education courses with other instructors, they were usually White males. I often felt I was an "extra" and not a real leader. Whether it was intentional or not, my voice was secondary. During my first wilderness educator training in the Tetons range in Wyoming, my dear mentor, Dr. Chris Cashel, found me lacking confidence in myself. On a crispy blue-sky morning, Chris held both of my shoulders, asked me to look into her eyes and to repeat the following phrase: "I'm an excellent leader." I was confused and didn't know how to react. No one in my life had told me this before Dr. Cashel. Culturally, being confident in my own capabilities was considered arrogant, but I couldn't disagree with my dear teacher. I felt my face get hot with embarrassment. All that my confused brain could offer was "ahhhh…, I guess I'm a good leader," but Chris was not happy with my unwilling response. Her eyes and voice demanded more from me. She said slowly, "Aiko, repeat after me: 'I AM AN EXCELLENT LEADER'!" After a little pause, I repeated what she said. The moment was so disorientating that I couldn't fully comprehend what she meant. In retrospect, this was the moment that cracked the asphalt binding my self-confidence and I became the wilderness educator I wanted to be.

Values

The mainstream U.S. outdoor adventure education philosophy is primarily based on Eurocentric middle- to upper-class values. This includes an emphasis on the primacy of individualism that contrasts with Japan's strongly collectivistic culture that values collective harmony over individual needs. This gap between my own collectivistic assumptions and the assumed primacy of individualism usually reveals itself during leadership experiences such as deciding which route to take, resolving members' conflicts when they feel unfairly treated by other group members, or working with an individual that is moving slower than the pace the other group members want to travel. This value difference altered the results of these negotiations as well as the decision-making process.

When individualism is assumed, such as in the United States context in my experience, an individual's personal identity and opinions are valued. Therefore, individuals are encouraged to speak up about their personal feelings and opinions. In contrast, in the collectivistic culture I grew up in and began working in outdoor education, more weight would be put on the idea of "selflessness or altruism." Rather than seeking to elevate the needs of the individual, the goal was to help people bend their individual needs and desires to be focused on the group goals and maintain social harmony. This difference in basic goals meant that I and my co-instructors were working towards fundamentally different goals. This led to developmental feedback based on the assumption that we were all working towards individualistic outcomes and left me feeling incompetent, isolated, and puzzled. It was like learning a group dance when I was hearing a very different song; it was not just about my ability to dance, but I was dancing to a different beat.

"The nail that sticks out gets hammered down" is a well-known Japanese proverb describing the process for maintaining conformity in Japanese society. However, the simplicity of this quip does not explain who sets the standard for which nails are sticking out and what level the other nails should be raised or lowered to. Growing up in the homogeneous collectivist society of Japan, I was taught by my family and society that I needed to abide by feminine values that included not being the nail that sticks out and to be submissive to the group's will. Rather than being encouraged to strongly communicate my individual perspective, I was told I needed to listen, laugh softly, feel thankful for any support I received from others, and avoid recognition for my individual strengths and achievements. To state the obvious, the previous sentence does not describe the idealized outdoor educator leading mainstream wilderness expeditions in the United States context I experienced as a nascent outdoor educator.

In the North American context, outdoor adventure education leaders are encouraged to share their outdoor experiences so that students (and employers) trust them to lead expeditions. Leaders are asked to express their perspective boldly and clearly. Looking at these actions through the cultural lens that I was raised with, these leaders would be considered egotistical and brash as opposed to the humble supportive leaders assumed to be the ideal in the Japanese context. I felt conflicted about unapologetically stating my opinions, assuming I could even identify my personal opinion. I had been trained to recognize and bend to the group's will, so making this switch was a very different goal. This was further problematized by my experience, both in the Japanese and North American contexts, that decisions would be made without my input. So why should I create animosity by introducing a conflicting opinion and ruffle the group harmony? My assumption was that I was to support rather than stand out as the recognized leader. Rather than practice self-care, I sacrificed the joy of being outdoors and my personal health to carry group gear. I considered self-care to be selfish and recognition to be embarrassing. A classic example is this. During a typical summer thunderstorm and heavy rain on the Olympic Mountain range in the evening, we were all exhausted and tired, as we came to our backcountry campsite. We were exhausted by long hikes and climbs, and this sudden cold front rolled in. The storm rapidly sucked the heat from our bodies and rapidly sent some group members from sweating to their teeth chattering and body shivering. As this progressed, I moved around to each student group to make sure they were properly setting up their tarps. I was so focused on this task that I had neglected to put on my own rain jacket. I got soaked by the sleet as I supported others. My thanks for this group support was feedback from the senior instructor that I had expressed poor judgment. My altruistic actions held little value and led to humiliation. To be a safe leader in certain outdoor situations, I had to learn to be more "selfish" (according to Japanese culture) and yet continue to nourish the values of servant leadership.

Chameleon?

My father once told me "When in Rome, do as the Romans do." This need to code-switch assumes a plasticity of action and values that may not always be possible. Surviving in wilderness education in the United States has required a certain level of assimilation to the dominant values and norms. In retrospect, I may have chosen to not adapt in certain ways if I was fully conscious of having a choice; however, that level of awareness is often a luxury of hindsight. Survival required consciously and unconsciously changing myself to fit in–how I looked, what I did, and even what I thought at times. I worked hard to be like my confident, experienced, and popular co-instructors. After several years in the workplace, the feedback I received from students, peers, and my employers suggested that I realized many of those aspects of the ideal (North American) outdoor education leader. But what did I lose in that process? Fortunately, or unfortunately, I lost my ability to recognize and bend to the group will without questioning how those norms were established, by who, and whether those were the correct goals to reach for.

In a sense, I lost what it means to be a Japanese woman. I no longer feel comfortable in the culture of the country I was raised in. These two decades of shifting values means that I no longer have a culture that I can comfortably fit into. In my experience, complete comfort in any cultural context requires a willful ignorance to the structure of assumptions that I can no longer sustain. When asked why I came to the US to study outdoor education, I can no longer reply that I wish to go back to Japan to create my own outdoor education organization. I have changed colors too much to revert to my previous shades. On the positive side, this process has fed my hunger to learn who I am, what I value, and how that compares to the values held by others. It feeds my curiosity as I make the journey of learning and to feel greater compassion for those that differ from me. My mission has shifted from developing competence to staying curious and compassionate.

Call for Action

Based on my own experience, these are the actions I would suggest others consider in their journey.

♦ Be sensitive to others' needs, cultural backgrounds, and beliefs that they may be uncomfortable communicating.

♦ Learn your own heritage and culture to a depth that allows you to identify the assumptions in your culture to enable you to ask why you believe what you do.

♦ Stay hungry for learning about others' cultural values and allow those values to help you further identify your own values.

♦ Place yourself in unfamiliar environments where you're a nondominant member so you can identify what aspects of culture you are assuming to be correct without realizing that this is even a choice.

♦ Create an inclusive group where each person brings their own cultural value and rituals and practices.

♦ Before judging others' actions ask yourself, and if needed, ask them politely and respectfully, "Why did you do what you did?" This can be an opportunity for both to learn more about themselves and others.

♦ Be aware of your own context-dependent unearned privileges and how that can oppress counterparts without not knowing it —in the United States context, identifying with dominant Eurocentric, upper/middle-class values are a privilege that may not be apparent to those experiencing it.

♦ Stay humble and stay curious.

References

Parker, Claire. (2022, June 3). Japan records its largest natural population decline as births fall. *The Washington Post.* https://www.washingtonpost.com/world/2022/06/03/japan-low-births-population-decline-2021

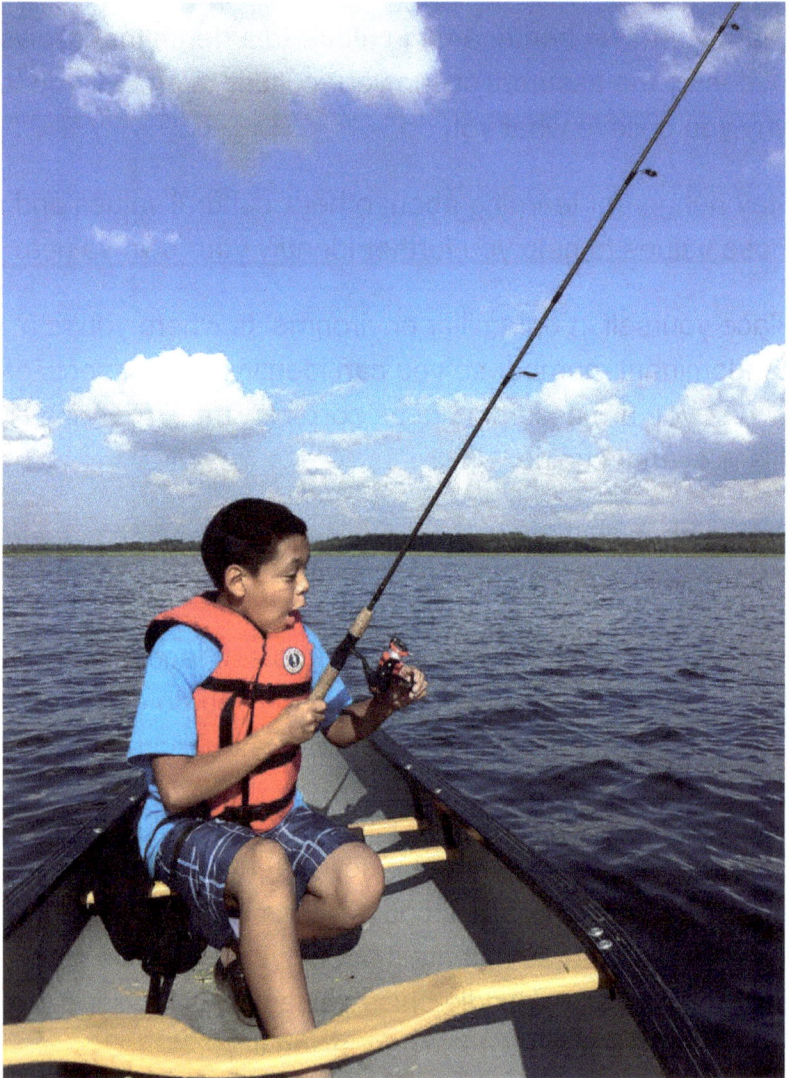

Photo courtesy of Lise Brown, Momenta

Nina Roberts: A Remembrance

Bill Gwaltney

In so many ways, the woman who became Dr. Nina Roberts was a force of nature. She possessed a personal connection to the out of doors and was possessed with a passion to share those places and wild spaces with everyone. Her personal and professional life was dedicated to sharing wild green spaces with the underserved and the urban. She was committed to connecting the historically forgotten populations to wild spaces and giving children of every age a connection to the history of wilderness and the legacy that every living human being is heir to.

Her life was about fairness. She was about making the very earth we walk on, the air we breathe, the water we drink, and the memories we share about the planet we live on more than a faint memory of a distant past but a real place to be protected, understood, and enjoyed.

She dedicated her professional career to understanding the historical, emotional, and social barriers that stood between wild places and green spaces and communities of color. She did so in an effort to tear down those barriers so that all Americans, all people, regardless of class, color, sexual orientation, educational level, background, or experience could feel and value the warmth of the planet that gave us life and sustains that life.

It did not take me long to get her hired as a Student Career Employment Program employee at the Intermountain Regional Office in Lakewood, Colorado, where she would work with me on diversity, hiring, and outreach programs for the National Park Service. Nina's passion for in-person training on topics related to diversity and the out of doors led to our involvement with a Diversity and the Outdoors Conference proposed and sponsored by Dr. Patty Limerick, who was already with the Center for the American West at Colorado State University.

All good things must come to an end, and Nina felt that she had to give more time and focus to the work that would result in her doctorate, so she left the National Park Service, but she and I would always remain close. Never letting her doctorate go to her head, Nina always looked for ways to make a difference on the ground as well as in the academic world. For her, experience was education, and education was experience. She gave literally dozens of presentations and NEVER did the same thing twice.

I was proud to share presentations with her on topics as divergent as "Critical Directions in the Interpretation of American Wilderness" at the National Association for Interpretation Annual Meeting in 2001. That panel discussion featured, at Nina's recommendation, commentary from the inimitable Jerry Stevens, a former Denver attorney and judge. Stevens had fallen from grace due to drug use, but he used his personal wilderness journey and the climbing of every 14,000-foot peak in Colorado to put the fog of drug use behind him.

In 2000, Nina and I shared the stage with Cheryl Armstrong from the Beckwourth Mountain Club in another presentation, "Innovative Strategies for Engaging and Respecting the Values and Interests of All Communities in National Parks and Landscapes." Based on the work I was doing at Rocky Mountain National Park, the presentation was done for the Mosaic in Motion 2000 Conference.

It was Nina who connected me with so many fantastic people, including Dr. Carolyn Finney, now at Middlebury College, Dr. Emilyn Sheffield, at California State University at Chico, and Dr. Don Rodriquez (now Professor at California State University

Channel Islands), who was Nina's graduate advisor and later colleague at Colorado State University.

As recently as 2019, I suggested that Dr. Roberts be invited as the keynote speaker for the National Association for Interpretation Annual Conference in Denver, Colorado. The title of her address was "Keeping Up & Keeping it Real!: Changes, Challenges, & Connections for Diversity, Access, & Inclusion for Youth and Nature."

Nina's focus on fairness, academic freedom, and human honesty were always on display, but they would come into razor sharp focus for me in a way I never expected. After being confronted and effectively silenced for using the "N-word" in a purposefully antiracist presentation, it was Nina Roberts who took the time to pen a detailed defense of my work and a thorough explanation of who she believed me to be and how censorship never helps anyone other than the oppressor.

Dr. Nina Roberts was first in many things, largely because she did the right thing first and put herself last. I traveled to San Francisco to be with Nina a few months ago. I took her to some of her medical appointments, helped her with chores, stocked her pantry, fed her, and placed prepared food in her freezer. While I was there, she was constantly on the phone and Zoom calls, attending to the needs of her research, her colleagues, and her graduate students.

When I returned home, having already seen critical changes in her health and appearance, I invited her to spend time with my wife and me in Hawaii, thinking it could cheer her spirit, even if it could do little for her body. Her dedication to the work she had taken on meant that she would postpone that trip until it was no longer possible.

It is easy to remember Nina's inspiration—her fire and her focus—and we would do well to also remember that above all things, Nina Roberts was fun. Her broad smile, her infectious laugh, and her joy in living are the inspirations we all need to carry forward her work, her message, and her commitment to connecting people to the planet. We can say of Dr. Nina Roberts what was said of Stephen T. Mather, the first director of the National Park Service: "There will never come an end to the good she has done."

Art courtesy of Duane Red Wolf Miles

Call to Action

Photo courtesy of Sherry Bagley

Call to Action

Sändra J. Washington and Sharon J. Washington

Talk is good. However, talking alone is not enough, and neither is reading stories enough. The only way to make a cultural shift towards greater equity and greater inclusion is with self-reflection and action.

The shift will come when more individuals (and institutions through them) recognize their part in perpetuating the status quo, and not even one of us is without some responsibility. We all play a part in the perpetuation of marginalization and injustice.

White women experience sexism and perpetuate racism. Immigrants in the United States experience xenophobia and perpetuate homophobia. BIPOC folx experience racism and other forms of marginalization and still perpetuate the same against other BIPOC folx and communities. Individually and collectively, we must be willing to look inside ourselves and be open to hearing the stories of others. Everyone wants to be seen, and the exchange of resilient listening is where understanding takes root.

The personal experiences shared highlight universal feelings of inadequacy, hope, disappointment, courage, fear, and love. We hope these shared stories spark conversations and dialogues that lead to greater understanding.

Tips for Facilitating Discussions

♦ Provide clear expectations for the discussion. Let the group members know if the expectation at the end of the discussion is for an action (e.g., increasing representation, policy change), to be taken or to gain greater understanding.

189

Discussions focused on deepening understanding of others' experiences can develop greater cognitive empathy and provide a richer context for taking further action.

◆ Offer shared agreements for the group. Ask the participants to take responsibility for the quality of their participation in the discussion.

◆ Ask folks to speak from their own perspectives, and not on behalf of others.

◆ Be conscious of "airtime", so everyone is heard and not just those who are quick to talk. If someone in the group is dominating the conversation, you may need to gently interrupt and make space for others to have an opportunity to speak.

◆ Provide time and space for quiet reflection. This may help those who need time to consider what they'd like to say and participate more readily in the conversation.

◆ These conversations can evoke strong emotions. As the facilitator, the more you understand the topics or the particular attributes that trigger an emotional response in you, the better equipped you'll be to manage your responses and understand the range of emotions that may be present.

◆ Assume good intentions, and acknowledge good intentions are different from the impact our words may have. If your words have a hurtful impact, apologize and commit to doing better. These conversations take practice; we are learning together.

We hope these personal reflections lead us to actions for greater fairness and inclusion in our workspaces and our interactions in the places where we find rejuvenation. The power of this field guide is the change it sparks in the world.

Suggested Reading List for Facilitating DEIB Discussions

Decety, J., & Yoder, K. J. (2016). Empathy and motivation for justice: Cognitive empathy and concern, but not emotional empathy, predict sensitivity to injustice for others. *Social Neuroscience, 11*(1), 1–14. https://www.ncbi.nlm.nih.gov/pmc/articles/PMC4592359/

Gurin, P., Nagda, B. R. A., Zúñiga, X. (2013), *Dialogue Across Differences: Practice, Theory, and Research on Intergroup Dialogue*, Russell Sage Foundation.

Maxwell, K. E., Biren (Ratnesh) A. Nagda, and Monita C. Thompson, (Eds.) (2011). *Facilitating Intergroup Dialogues: Bridging Differences, Catalyzing Change*. Stylus Publishing.

Resilient Communication https://brainalchemist.com/2013/02/14/5-practices-for-resilient-communication/

Cognitive Empathy vs. Emotional Empathy - Verywell Mind https://www.verywellmind.com/cognitive-and-emotional-empathy-4582389

Together One Lincoln https://togetheronelincoln.org/conversation/

Guide to Facilitating Dialogues https://diversity.missouri.edu/wp-content/uploads/2018/07/facilitating-dialogue.pdf

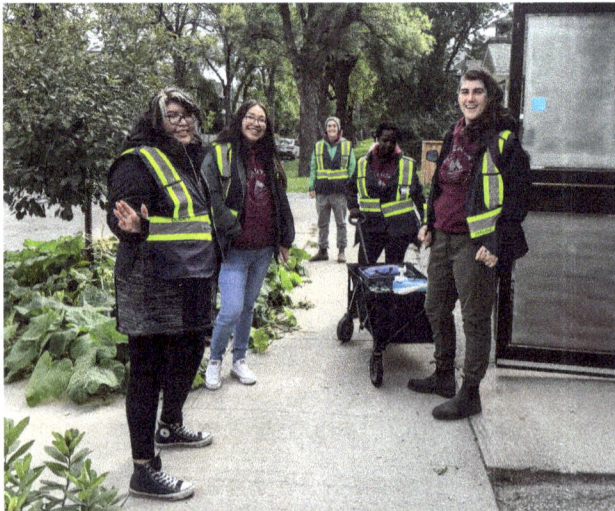

Photo courtesy of Lise Brown, Momenta

Definition of Terms

Photo courtesy of the Roberts Family

Definition of Terms

The definitions included in this field guide are to enable leaders, facilitators, instructors, and readers to understand and use terms that are often associated with social justice. Definitions of these terms were adapted with permission from Foundation for a Healthy St. Petersburg, Ongig, The Avarna Group, The Safe Zone Project, and World Trust. The field guide project members acknowledge Black Equality Resources, the Climate Action Network International, The Latina Feminist Group, The Merriam-Webster Dictionary, The National Institutes of Health, Wikipedia, World Health organization, and other sources were also used and incorporated. This list is not meant to be exhaustive—it primarily represents terms used in this field guide. Definitions associated with diversity, equity, inclusion, and belonging evolve. Therefore, over time, some of these definitions may change or may be different from a reader's preferred definition.

Ability is the quality or state of being able (including physically and cognitively) as well as having the power, skill, means, or opportunity to do something.

Ableism can refer to either individual or institutional actions and language that disadvantage or disempower people with disabilities, people experiencing disabilities, or disabled people. Ableism can target mental, physical, and emotional disabilities as well as people who are neurodiverse.

Affinity bias describes unconscious preferences many people have for people who are more like them.

Affinity groups are a collection of individuals with similar interests or goals. Affinity groups promote inclusion, diversity, and other efforts that benefit people from underrepresented groups. Affinity groups can made up of groups such as employees, organizational members, and students.

Affinity spaces are places where affinity groups can safely congregate.

Afro-Caribbean is a person of African descent born or living in a Caribbean nation.

Ageism refers to the stereotypes (how we think), prejudice (how we feel) and discrimination (how we act) towards others or oneself based on age.

Agender means not having a gender. Some agender people describe it as a "lack of gender," while others describe themselves as being gender neutral. People use genderless or genderfree to mean more or less the same thing.

Ally(ies) is person who makes the commitment and effort to recognize and eliminate their privilege (based on gender, class, race, sexual identity, etc.) and work in solidarity with oppressed people in the struggle for justice. Allies understand that it is in their interest to end all forms of oppression, even those from which they may benefit in direct or indirect ways.

Allyship is a philosophy rooted in action; it demands doing what is necessary to recognize and subvert systems of oppression. Allyship is a process, is based on trust and accountability, looks different for everyone based on their identities, experiences, and spheres of influence, and is not self-defined (i.e., you don't label yourself as an "ally"). Allyship has been critiqued as being too passive and replaced by accompliceship and coconspirator. For a more robust discussion of this topic see the article "Accomplices not Allies" as well as www.whiteaccomplices.org.

Androgyne is a term for a person identifying gender outside of the gender binary. Androgynous is a gender expression that has elements of both masculinity and femininity. It is occasionally used in place of "intersex" to describe a person with both female and male anatomy, generally in the form "androgyne."

Antiracism is the consistent practice of identifying and challenging racist (system of advantage based on race) actions and ideas. This work is accomplished by changing systems, organizational structures, policies and practices, and attitudes and by redistributing power in a racially equitable manner.

Antiracist is someone who supports policies that seek to dismantle advantages based on race through their actions or expressing ideas

194

against such systems. This includes the expression that racial groups are equals and support of policies that reduce racial inequity.

Apartheid means racial segregation—specifically a former policy of segregation and political, social, and economic discrimination against the nonwhite majority in the Republic of South Africa.

Asian is a native or inhabitant of Asia or a person of Asian descent.

Asian-American is a person who has origins in Asia or the Indian subcontinent. Asian-American includes people who live in the United States and indicate their race as: Asian, Indian, Chinese, Filipino, Korean, Japanese, Vietnamese, Other Asian countries.

Bias is prejudice in favor of or against a thing, person, or group compared with another, usually in a way considered to be unfair. Unconscious or implicit bias refers to biases that people carry without awareness.

BIPOC (Pronounced "by pock") is an acronym for Black, Indigenous, and People of Color that is more specific than the term "People of Color." It is used to emphasize that experiences of discrimination and prejudice vary among People of Color. The term BIPOC enables a shift from terms such as "marginalized" and "minority" which denote inferiority. The term, used since the early 2010s, has gained popularity on social media, especially in the United States. Although the term highlights Black and Indigenous peoples, it is also important whenever possible to identify people through their own racial or ethnic group, as each has its own distinct experience and meaning and may be more appropriate, e.g., one would not use the term 'BIPOC' if solely referring to Black people. While BIPOC is thought to be an inclusive term for people not identifying as White many people outside of the United States not identifying as White do not choose to use this term.

Black means to be related to people who have ethnic origins in Africa, or not of White European descent. In the United States, Black is often used interchangeably with African American.

Black, Indigenous and People of Color (BIPOC)—See BIPOC

Capitalism is an economic system characterized by private or corporate ownership of capital goods and by investments that are determined by private decision. Capitalism has been criticized for prioritizing profit over social good, natural resources, and the environment as well as for establishing power in the hands of a minority capitalist class that exists through the exploitation of a working-class majority and for being an engine of inequality and economic instabilities.

Capitalist patriarchy describes the mutually reinforcing dialectical relationship between capitalist class structure and hierarchical gender structuring. Vandana Shiva notes the destructiveness and antilife ideology of capitalist patriarchy towards nonindustrial, noncapitalist, and Indigenous cultures.

Christian describes a person who professes belief in the teachings of Jesus Christ.

Cisgender is a person whose gender identity is consistent with the sex they were assigned at birth (e.g., a person assigned female at birth identifies as a woman).

Class refers to how much wealth a person has access to through property, inheritance, family support, investments, or other wealth not directly associated to wage earning.

Classism is to have prejudicial thoughts or to discriminate against a person or group based on differences in access to wealth, socioeconomic status, or income level.

Climate action is taking urgent and sustainable action to tackle the climate crisis and to achieve social and racial justice.

Code-switching is the practice of altering behavior, appearance, and language to fit in with a different group of people. Codeswitching happens for many reasons. In the DEIB context, code-switching typically refers to the practice by people with marginalized identities changing their behavior, appearance, and language to assimilate to the dominant culture and gain access to advantages experienced by people with dominant identities.

Collectivism is a political or economic theory advocating collective control especially over production and distribution.

Colonial history is the history of **colonialism**, which is a practice or policy of control by one people or power over other people or areas. This control often happens by establishing colonies, generally with the aim of economic dominance or genocide. In the process of colonization, colonizers may impose their religion, language, economics, and other cultural practices.

Colonization refers to forms of invasion, dispossession, or control of an underrepresented group (e.g., when European people invaded the United States and committed near genocide to the Native Americans).

Colorblindness is a concept in which a person believes that ignoring the existence of race or skin color in service of seeing past race and just seeing the person helps achieve equality. This de-emphasizing of race, however, ignores the real, lived experience of People of Color in the United States and globally. This term is ableist in that it diminishes the experiences of people who are blind or experience visual impairments.

Colored people (or coloured) is a racial descriptor historically used in the United States during the Jim Crow Era to refer to African American people. It was also used as a descriptor in Southern Africa.

Comfort zone is often meant to describe a psychological state in which a person is at ease, experiencing low levels of anxiety and stress, because they perceive themselves to be in control of their environment. Brené Brown describes it as "Where our uncertainty, scarcity and vulnerability are minimized—where we believe we'll have access to enough love, food, talent, time, admiration. Where we feel we have some control."

Confirmation bias describes humans' tendency to interpret information based on a way that confirms their previous beliefs and experiences.

Cultural competence(y) describes the ability to interact effectively across various facets of diversity, to flex with differences. Cultural competence is what people need to be inclusive. It requires a) being self-aware of your own culture, assumptions, values, styles, biases, attitudes, privilege, and such; b) understanding others' cultures,

197

assumptions, values, styles, biases, attitudes, privilege, and such; and c) based on this knowledge, understanding your potential impact on others and interacting with them in situationally appropriate ways.

Cultural humility is a lifelong process of self-reflection and self-critique whereby individuals start with an examination of their own beliefs and cultural identities as they learn about others' cultures. Key attributes of cultural humility include openness, self-awareness, lifelong learning, empathy and compassion, ability to be other-oriented, institutional accountability, and acknowledgment of and balancing of power imbalances.

Cultural pluralism means recognition of the contribution of each group of people to the common civilization. It encourages the maintenance and development of different lifestyles, languages, and convictions. Cultural pluralism includes a commitment to work cooperatively with common concerns. People strive to create the condition of harmony and respect within a culturally diverse society.

Cultural racism is the individual and institutional expression of the superiority of one race's cultural heritage and values over another.

Culture describes the sum total of ways of living, including values, beliefs, aesthetic standards, linguistic expression, patterns of thinking, behavioral norms, and styles of communication that a group of people has developed to assure its survival in a particular environment. We are socialized through "cultural conditioning" to adopt ways of thinking related to societal grouping. This set of shared ideas, customs, traditions, beliefs, and practices constantly changes in subtle and major ways.

DEI abbreviates diversity, equity, and inclusion.

DEIB abbreviates diversity, equity, inclusion, and belonging.

Decolonize is the active resistance against colonial powers from Indigenous people and culture groups.

Disability is a social construct. The mental, emotional, and physical norms that determine what is different or what is a disability are arbitrary. Ability can be visualized as a spectrum with people who are extremely physically and mentally capable at one end and disabled at the other end. Trying to define the line between abled and disabled can be difficult. As people age they migrate towards the disabled side of the spectrum.

Discrimination is the behavioral manifestation of prejudice involving limiting opportunities and options of others based on criterion such as race, gender, sex, age, class, body size, ability, immigration status, and family structure.

Diversity is a goal of inclusion and equity efforts. Race and ethnicity are one way in which people are diverse as a group. There are countless more visible and invisible facets of diversity including abilities, age, disabilities, learning styles, life experiences, neurodiversity, class, gender, sexual orientation, country of origin, and cultural, political, or religious affiliation. Diversity can be the differences among people from which they experience systemic advantages or encounter systemic barriers in access to opportunities and resources. A person cannot be "diverse" (as in a "diverse candidate").

Dominant culture refers to the cultural beliefs, values, and traditions that are based on those of a dominant society. Dominant culture practices are usually considered "normal" and "right" by dominant people in that culture.

Equality in the context of diversity is typically defined as treating everyone the same and giving everyone access to the same opportunities. It is sometimes used as an alternative to "inclusion."

Equity, an approach based in fairness, ensures everyone has access to the same opportunities and resources. Equity therefore, is not the same thing as equality. Equity seeks to balance disparities from people having different access to resources because of systems of oppression and privilege. In practice, equity ensures everyone is given equal opportunity to thrive, meaning that resources may be divided and shared unequally to make sure that each person can access an opportunity.

Ethnicity refers to a group of people who identify with one another based on characteristics such as shared culture, cultural heritage, and ancestral geographic base.

Ethnocentrism means to apply one's own culture or ethnicity as a frame of reference to judge other cultures, practices, behaviors, beliefs, and people, instead of using the standards of the particular culture involved. It is the attitude that one's own group, ethnicity, or nationality is superior to others.

Euro-centric means to centered on Europe or the Europeans—especially reflecting a tendency to interpret the world in terms of European or Anglo-American values and experiences.

Feminism is a range of socio-political movements and ideologies based on the belief in and advocacy of the political, economic, and social equality of all people. It was first seen as between the sexes and expressed through organized activity on behalf of women's rights and interests. It is now seen as inclusion and equality of all genders and the earth.

Feminist describes a person who supports or engages in feminism.

Folx is an umbrella term for all people with special inclusion for people of non-normative gender, sexual orientation, or identity.

Gaslighting is the psychological manipulation of a person usually over an extended period that causes the victim to question the validity of their own thoughts, perception of reality, or memories and typically leads to confusion, loss of confidence and self-esteem, uncertainty of one's emotional or mental stability, and a dependency on the perpetrator.

Gay is a contested umbrella term used to refer to people who experience a same-sex or same-gender attraction. Many women attracted to women do not use the term gay to describe themselves. Gay is also an identity term used to describe a male-identified person who is attracted to other male-identified people in a romantic, sexual, and/or emotional sense.

Gay-straight has been used as a binary to describe sexuality. It is often used in Gay–Straight Alliance, Gender- Sexuality Alliance or Queer–Straight Alliance to describe a student-led or community-based organization, found in middle schools, high schools, colleges, and universities. These support organizations are primarily in the United States and Canada.

Gender is a term used to describe socially constructed roles, behaviors, activities, and attributes that society considers "appropriate" for men and women. It is separate from sex, which is the biological classification of male or female based on physiological and biological features.

Gender binary is the false assumption that there are only two genders, women and men.

Gender expression or presentation is the way that someone outwardly displays their gender through clothing, style, demeanor, and behavior.

Gender identity is how a person self identifies their gender including being agender. There are countless ways in which people may identify or gender themselves including agender, gender fluid, gender queer, man, nonbinary, trans, two spirit, woman.

Gender neutral, or gender neutrality, describes policies, language, and other social institutions that avoid distinguishing roles based on sex or gender. A gender neutral word or expression is one that cannot be taken to refer to a particular gender. These might include two-person tent, firefighter, police officer, flight attendant. Being gender neutral helps avoid discrimination.

Gender-neutral pronouns are words that don't specify whether the subject of the sentence is a boy or a girl or a man or a woman. 'They', for instance, is a third-person pronoun that is gender neutral. Other gender-neutral pronouns include 'them', 'this person', 'everyone', 'Ze', or 'Hir'. If you're not sure which pronoun to use, you can also use that person's name. APA for scholarly papers encourages gender neutral pronouns—especially if the person's gender or preferred pronouns are unknown. Using gender neutral pronouns can help create inclusive learning, work, and social spaces.

Gendered is used as a modifier in that a gendered profession is mostly done by people of one gender. A gendered behavior is behavior that is strongly associated with a gender.

Genderfluid describes a person who does not defined themself as having a fixed gender. Their gender identity varies over time. It may be a dynamic mix of traits typically considered masculine and feminine. A person who is genderfluid may feel like a mix of men, women, and other genders, but may feel more masculine some days, and more feminine other days.

Genderqueer describes a person whose gender identity or gender expression does not align with conventional gender distinctions such as the gender binary.

Gender washed (**washing**) describes actions that appear to be more woman or girl-friendly or more accepting of unconventional gender identities than they actuality are. For example, companies can be merely performative in their embracement of women and girls or unconventional gender identities.

Glass ceiling describes an intangible barrier within a hierarchy that prevents women or other marginalized people from obtaining upper-level positions.

Hegemonic describes the social, cultural, ideological, or economic influence exerted by a dominant group in a society.

Heterosexism is the belief that heterosexuality is superior or "normal" compared to other forms of sexuality, sexual orientation, or sexual expression.

Heterosexual describes a person attracted to the opposite sex or gender (e.g., a woman-identified person who is attracted to a man-identified person).

Homogeneous means of the same or a similar kind or nature.

Homophobia is to have an irrational fear or intolerance of people who are homosexual or having feelings of homosexuality.

Human rights refer to rights (such as freedom from unlawful imprisonment, torture, and execution) regarded as belonging fundamentally to all persons. These include the right to access clean water and food.

Identity distinguishes the character or personality of an individual. Examples of social identities are ability, age, gender, race or ethnicity, religion or religious beliefs, sexual orientation, and social class or socioeconomic status.

Imperialism is the policy, practice, or advocacy of extending the power and dominion of a nation especially by direct territorial acquisitions or by gaining indirect control over the political or economic life of people in other areas.

Imposter syndrome can be described a collection of feelings of inadequacy that persist despite evident success. People with imposter syndrome suffer from chronic self-doubt and a sense of intellectual fraudulence that override feelings of success or external proof of their competence. As an example, members of under-represented groups can be unable to internalize their accomplishments (imposter syndrome) because of biases and gaslighting. These competent individuals are in constant fear of being exposed as a fraud.

Inclusion is exemplified by celebrating, centering, and amplifying the perspectives, voices, values, and needs of people who experience systemic barriers, mistreatment, or disadvantages based on their identities to ensure they feel a sense of belonging. Inclusion is not merely tolerating or accommodating differences, it's about actively valuing and honoring differences.

Indigenous people, also known as First Peoples, First Nations, Aboriginal peoples, Native peoples, or autochthonous peoples are ethnic groups who are descended from and identify with the original inhabitants of a given region, in contrast to groups that have settled, occupied, or colonized the area more recently.

Individualism favors freedom of action for individuals over collective or state control. In the United States encouragement has been given to individualism, free enterprise, and the pursuit of profit over many people's basic needs and over dismantling White supremacy and racism.

Institutional racism, also known as systemic racism is a form of racism that is embedded in the laws and regulations, customs, traditions, and practices of a society or an organization. This racism manifests as discrimination in areas such as criminal justice, employment, housing, health care, education, and political representation.

203

Internal & external frameworks refer to the internal structures and neural pathways formed in the brain that respond to, and a way of, making meaning of the history, culture, and identity formation that pervade and inform what is considered normal. These frameworks may be part of, and responded to in ways that are unconscious or deeply inform assumptions related to one's worldview. They are associated with conscious and unconscious bias, privilege, and internalized racism. These nested elements are more than personal. They impact behaviors that are individual, collective, and relational. These belief systems inform external relationships that are interpersonal, institutional, and structural and are mechanisms for inequities.

Internalized racism is the personal conscious or subconscious acceptance of the dominant society's racist views, stereotypes, and biases of one's ethnic group. It gives rise to patterns of thinking, feeling, and behaving that result in discriminating, minimizing, criticizing, finding fault, invalidating, and hating oneself while simultaneously valuing the dominant culture.

Internalized oppression is the internalization of conscious or unconscious attitudes regarding inferiority or differences by the victims of systematic oppression.

Interpersonal racism are beliefs and actions that perpetuate inequalities on the basis of race. Such behaviors may be intentional or unintentional.

Interracial is of, involving, or designed for members of different races.

Intersectionality, a term used by feminist legal scholar Kimberlé Crenshaw, to account for the ways in which Black women experience both racism and sexism. It has now expanded to account for the ways that an individual can experience multiple forms of oppression based on multiple marginalized identities.

Isms is a way of describing any attitude, action, or institutional structure that subordinates (oppresses) a person or group because of their target group's color (racism), ability (ableism), size (sizeism), economic status (classism), gender (sexism), sexual orientation (heterosexism), gender identity (cissexism), older age (ageism), youth (adultism), religion (e.g., antisemitism), language or immigrant status (nativism), and so forth.

JEDI abbreviates justice, equity, diversity, and inclusion.

Justice involves dismantling systems of oppression and privilege that create systemic disadvantages and barriers to people's ability to access resources and opportunities. Through systems of oppression and privilege people experience systemic mistreatment. Whereas equity is about reapportioning or redistributing resources so people can access opportunities, justice is about dismantling barriers to those opportunities.

Latina refers to a woman or girl who descended from or is a native or inhabitant of Latin America.

Latinos refer to people who are from or descended from people from Latin America.

Latinx is a gender-neutral term to replace Latino or Latina when referring to a person of Latin-American descent.

Lesbian refers to a woman-identified person who is attracted emotionally, physically, or sexually to other woman-identified people.

Lesbian baiting is the sexist and homophobic practice of labeling women (especially feminists and women whose behavior doesn't reinforce traditional gender stereotypes) as lesbian in an effort to slur or diminish them.

LGBT abbreviates lesbian, gay, bisexual, and transgender and is often used to encompass sexual preference and gender identities that do not correspond to heterosexual norms). There are multiple variations of LGBT to increase inclusivity as follows:

LGBTQ – Lesbian, gay, bisexual, transgender, and queer (or questioning).

LGBTQIA – Lesbian, gay, bisexual, transgender, queer (or questioning), intersex, and asexual (or agender, aromantic, allies).

LGBTA – Lesbian, gay, bisexual, transgender, and asexual/aromantic/agender.

LGBTIQQ – Lesbian, gay, bisexual, transgender, intersex, queer, and questioning.

LGBTTTQQIAA or LGBTQAI2+ – Lesbian, gay, bisexual, transgender, queer (or questioning), agender, intersex, and two-spirited. The "+" signifies other identities known and not known and can be used to keep the abbreviation brief when written out.

Living wage describes a wage sufficient to provide necessities and comforts essential to an acceptable standard of living.

Mansplain(ing) describes men explaining something to a person (typically a woman) in a condescending, overconfident and often inaccurate, or patronizing manner.

Marginalization means to exclude, ignore, or relegate a group of people to an unimportant or powerless position in organizations, groups, or society.

Marginalized communities or groups are people who face systemic disadvantages, exclusion, and barriers to opportunities, resources, and power based on their identities, including but not limited to poor and low-income communities, Black, Indigenous, and People of Color, immigrants, refugees, people with disabilities, women, anybody who identifies outside or beyond the gender binary or not as cisgender, and anybody who is not heterosexual.

Microaggressions are unconscious and conscious everyday behaviors that can disempower someone based on a marginalized identity (real or perceived). They can feel small or subtle to the person engaging in the microaggression—even when it is pointed out to them, but the impact can be large for the recipient. If experienced chronically, a person can feel, "death by a thousand tiny cuts."

Minority(ies) is a linguistical, mathematical, and historically irresponsible term used to describe racially, ethnically, or culturally distinct groups. It describes the wrong dynamic (marginalized people or underrepresented people are not lesser than—minor), is demographically in accurate, and ignores centrality of so many diverse groups in our history.

Misogyny refers to the hatred of, aversion to, or prejudice against women.

Mixed-race can mean a person who has parents who belong to different racial or ethnic groups.

Modern racism/racialization suggests that the culture of racial prejudice in the United States has changed. Many people currently use nonrace related reasons to continue to deny Black and other People of Color equal access to opportunities.

Multicultural education is a structured process designed to foster understanding, acceptance, and constructive relations among people of many different cultures. It encourages people to see many different cultures as a source of learning and to respect diversity in local, national, and international environments. Multicultural education helps people build an awareness of their own cultural heritage to understand that no one culture is intrinsically superior to another; secondly, it helps people acquire skills in analysis and communication that help them function effectively in multicultural environments.

Natives, Africans, Asians, Latinos & Allies is a subgroup of the Association for Experiential Education.

Native American is a broad term generally used to describe the Indigenous people from the United States. It refers to people of North and South America. Native American is often used interchangeably with American Indian, although many Native Americans find the word "Indian" offensive and prefer to identify themselves by their specific nation or tribe.

Neurodivergent refers to people whose cognitive functions work in ways that diverge from the dominant societal standards of "normal."

Nonbinary is a term used to describe people whose identifies do not exclusively fall into the binary gender classification of a man or a woman. Nonbinary can include people who identify as agender, with a gender that is not exclusively man or woman, or in between genders. It is sometime written as or abbreviated as enby, enbies, NB, or NBi.

Non-normative implies not conforming to or employing common norms.

207

Oppression is the systematic mistreatment of people by more powerful people, resulting in the targeting of certain groups within the society to receive less of its benefits. Oppression involves a subtle devaluing or nonacceptance of certain groups in terms of economic, political, social, and /or psychological aspects with the goal of taking their power away. Oppression includes the belief of superiority or "righteousness" of the group in power.

Paradigms are ways of organizing and condensing sensory information. A paradigm is a way of seeing the world. A paradigm shift often means someone's core values or approach to life have changed. Sometimes participation in outdoor programs results in a paradigm shift for participants.

Parkies is an informal name for workers in the National Park Service.

Patriarchy describes the institutionalization of men and/or masculinity as dominant over women and/or femininity in both the private and public spheres, such as the home, political, sports, and religious and social institutions. Patriarchy shapes and is shaped by White supremacy and capitalism.

People of Color (POC) – See BIPOC

Personal racism describes individual attitudes regarding the inferiority of one group and the superiority of another that have been learned or internalized either directly (e.g., negative experiences) or indirectly (e.g., imitation and modeling of significant others' reactions, affective responses to the media). These attitudes may be conscious or unconscious.

Prejudice describes a negative attitude toward a person or group, based on prejudgment and evaluation, often using one's own or one's group's standards as the "right" and "only" way.

Privilege could be considered the flip side of oppression. Privilege constitutes advantages people receive, consciously or unconsciously, by virtue of one or more of their identities. These advantages are upheld by systems of power that advantage certain group over others, and include ideologies such as racism, sexism, cissexism, heterosexism, elitism, classism, ableism, nativism, colonialism, ageism, and sizeism (collectively "the isms"). Privilege is the freedom from stress, anxiety, and fear of harm related to identity.

Power and economics describe the engines that "drive" a system (e.g., capitalism) that provides a rationale and elements of cognitive dissonance that is divisive.

Queer is an umbrella term that allows nonheterosexual people to identify their sexual orientation without stating who they are attracted to. The term queer can include gay men, lesbians, bisexuals, and transgendered people, though people in all these groups may contest having the word queer applied to them.

Race is a false construct that conflates skin color and ancestry with behavior, intelligence, and culture. Though false, it has real consequences for all people and cannot be ignored.

Racism describes the systematic oppression of People of Color. It occurs at the individual, internalized, interpersonal, institutional, and cultural levels and may be overt or covert, intentional or unintentional.

Radical feminists challenge existing social norms and institutions and seek to abolish the patriarchy as one front in a struggle to liberate everyone from an unjust society. This struggle includes opposing the sexual objectification of women. Radical feminism is a perspective within feminism that calls for a reordering of society in which male supremacy is eliminated in all social and economic contexts, while recognizing that women's experiences are also affected by other social divisions such as in race, class, and sexual orientation. Alice Walker, Andrea Dworkin, and bell hooks may be described as radical feminists. Barbara Smith describes herself as a radical Black lesbian feminist—see the Combahee River Collective—as do many other Black radical feminists.

Religious oppression is the systematic mistreatment of an individual or a group of individuals as a response to their religious beliefs, affiliations, or their lack thereof (e.g., antisemitism).

Romantic orientation describes an affinity for someone that evokes the desire to engage in an emotionally intimate relationship often based on the gender relationship between the person and the people they are romantically attracted to.

Separatism is the advocacy of cultural, ethnic, tribal, religious, racial, governmental, or gender separation from the larger group.

Sex or biological/natal sex is a term used to classify individuals as male, female, or intersex (often at birth or based on an ultrasound) based on their chromosomal, hormonal, and anatomical characteristics.

Sexism is prejudice or discrimination based on one's sex or gender. Sexism can affect anyone, but it primarily affects women and girls. It has been linked to stereotypes and gender roles. It often includes the belief that one's sex or gender is intrinsically superior to another. There is greater prestige afforded to masculine traits within the outdoor education fields and use of gendered language continues to be common in mainstream programs.

Sexual orientation refers to the type of attraction one feels for others, often described based on the gender relationship between the person and people they are sexually attracted to.

Social construct refers to an idea that has been created and accepted by the people in a society.

Socio-economic status refers to the amount of money one earns in wages, which can change rapidly.

Social injustice refers to wrongful actions against individuals or groups within society. These actions can infringe upon a group's or individual's rights, marginalize their opportunities, or treat them unfairly.

Social justice is the view that everyone deserves equal economic, political, and social rights, and opportunities. Social justice includes intentional steps that move society in the direction of equality, support for diversity, economic justice, participatory democracy, environmental harmony, and waging and resolving conflicts nonviolently.

Social mores are norms that are widely observed within a particular society. They can represent what is considered morally acceptable or unacceptable in a culture. Mores are socially constructed and do not necessarily represent ethical behavior.

Stereotypes describe the widely held, often exaggerated, oversimplified ideas and assumptions people hold about a person or group of people based on their identities (real or perceived). Usually, based on popular opinion, or misinformation, stereotypes (negative, neutral, or seemingly positive ones) are hurtful because they generalize that everyone in a certain group shares the same characteristics and function to maintain dysfunctional systems.

Structural racism/racialization refers to a system of social structures that produces cumulative, durable, race-based inequalities. It is also a method of analysis that is used to examine how historical legacies, individuals, structures, and institutions work interactively to distribute material and symbolic advantages and disadvantages along racial lines. Racialized outcomes do not require racist actors.

Systemic or institutional racism refers to policies and practices that generate different outcomes for persons of different racial groups. These laws, policies, and practices are not necessarily explicit in mentioning any racial group but create advantages for White persons and disadvantages for People of Color.

Testimonio is a first-person narration of a socially significant experience where the narrative voice metonymically represents others who have lived through similar situations. It can be used as a method to call attention to social injustices methodology, including a research methodology.

Third gender refers to a category of people who do not identify as women or men, but rather as neither, both, or a combination of men and women genders.

Tokenism is a practice of including one or a few members of an underrepresented group in a team or company, usually with no changes in policies, practices, or attitudes.

Transgender refers to a person whose gender identity and sometimes expression is different from the sex they were assigned at birth. Trans* is an umbrella term (contested by some people) that refers to various ways that people identify differently than their biological sex.

Trans men is an identity label sometimes adopted by female-to-male transgender people or transsexuals to signify that they are men while still affirming their history as assigned female sex at birth. Sometimes people use the term transguy.

Trans women is an identity label sometimes adopted by male-to-female transsexuals or transgender people to signify that they are women while still affirming their history as assigned male sex at birth.

Transphobia is a fear, hatred, or discrimination towards people who identify as transgender.

Unconscious bias describes unconscious, subtle, involuntary assumptions or judgments people make every day based on their prior experiences and culture.

Underrepresented describes a subset of a population with a smaller percentage of representation in groups than the general population. For example, women, People of Color, or Indigenous people can be described as a subset of the larger population and they are often underrepresented in organizations, on board of directors, and such.

Underserved describes a condition where people are provided with inadequate service—often regarding basic needs such as food, medical care, and social services.

White means of or relating to any of various population groups considered as having light pigmentation of the skin NOTE: The meaning of White as it relates to population groups has historically been fluid, with people of particular ancestries being excluded for a time before being included, and vice versa. Specific parameters are, however, sometimes set, as in the U.S. 2020 Census, which stipulates that "the category of 'White' includes all individuals who identify with one or more nationalities or ethnic groups originating in Europe, the Middle East, or North Africa." White is preferred over Caucasian, which has racist origins.

White privilege represents unearned advantages, privileges, or benefits given to people based solely on being White.

White savior complex describes the action in which a White person, or more broadly a White culture, attempts to "rescue" People of Color from a negative situation—often a system created by systemic racism.

White supremacy is institutionally perpetuated, historical, and an ever-evolving system of exploitation and oppression of continents, nations, and Peoples of Color that consolidates and maintains power and resources among White people. This system promotes the ideology of Whiteness as the standard and the belief that White people are superior to other races.

Women are people who self-identify as a woman. It describes a gender. Historically, and in current purported definitions a woman is described as an adult person born female—this definition is limited. Two X chromosomes or female sex organs are about biological sex, not gender.

Women-identifying refers to a person who identifies as a woman. It also can mean a person who identifies as a lesbian (see lesbian). Use women-identifying rather than female to be inclusive. Not everyone born or biologically a female is a woman and not every woman was born female.

Worldview means the way an individual perceives their relationship to the world (e.g., nature, other people, animals, institutions, objects, the cosmos, their creator). One's memories, expectations, assumptions, beliefs, attitudes, values, interests, past experiences, strong feelings, and prejudices, influence their worldview.

Xenophobia describes a fear and hatred of strangers or foreigners or of anything that is strange or foreign.

Social Justice Quotes

Photo courtesy of Karen Warren

Social Justice Quotes

As readers use these quotes note that the field guide project members strove to include access information. However, URLs and links change so be ready to enjoy an internet adventure if you need to trace the source.

"Our struggle today is not to have a female Einstein get appointed as an assistant professor. It is for a woman schlemiel to get as quickly promoted as a male schlemiel."—**Bella Abzug**, Women and Government: New Ways to Political Power

"We are all creative, but by the time we are three or four years old, someone has knocked the creativity out of us. Some people shut up the kids who start to tell stories. Kids dance in their cribs, but someone will insist they sit still. By the time the creative people are ten or twelve, they want to be like everyone else."—**Maya Angelou**

"Courage is the most important of all the virtues, because without courage you can't practice any other virtue consistently. You can practice any virtue erratically, but nothing consistently without courage."—**Maya Angelou**, https://news.cornell.edu/stories/2008/05/courage-most-important-virtue-maya-angelou-tells-seniors

"Do the best you can until you know better. Then when you know better, do better."—**Maya Angelou**, http://www.passiton.com

"I want American history taught. Unless I'm in that book, you're not in it either. History is not a procession of illustrious people. It's about what happens to a people. Millions of anonymous people is what history is about."—**James Baldwin**, https://wamu.org/story/17/02/05/did-i-get-james-baldwin-wrong/

"The defect of equality is that we only desire it with our superiors."—**Henry Becque**, https://www.forbes.com/quotes/3947/

"There is no way to repress pleasure and expect liberation, satisfaction, or joy."—**Adrienne Marie Brown** (2019), *Pleasure Activism: The politics of feeling good*, AK Press

"In a society that functions optimally, those who can should naturally want to provide for those who can't. That's how it's designed to work. I truly believe we're here to take care of one another."—**LeVar Burton**, https://www.azquotes.com/author/28042-LeVar_Burton

"Prisons do not disappear social problems, they disappear human beings."—**Angela Davis**, Colby, J. (September 14, 2018) 10 Angela Davis Quotes That Will Inspire Anyone To Keep Fighting for Social Injustice, Theblackdetour.com.

"I believe profoundly in the possibilities of democracy, but democracy needs to be emancipated from capitalism. As long as we inhabit a capitalist democracy, a future of racial equality, gender equality, economic equality will elude us."—**Angela Davis**, Colby, J. (September 14, 2018) 10 Angela Davis Quotes That Will Inspire Anyone To Keep Fighting for Social Injustice, Theblackdetour.com.

"The 13th amendment to the constitution of the US which abolished slavery – did not abolish slavery for those convicted of a crime."—**Angela Davis**, Colby, J. (September 14, 2018) 10 Angela Davis Quotes That Will Inspire Anyone To Keep Fighting for Social Injustice, Theblackdetour.com.

"In this society, dominated as it is by the profit-seeking ventures of monopoly corporations, health has been callously transformed into a commodity – a commodity that those with means are able to afford, but that is too often entirely beyond the reach of others."—**Angela Davis**, Colby, J. (September 14, 2018) 10 Angela Davis Quotes That Will Inspire Anyone To Keep Fighting for Social Injustice, Theblackdetour.com.

"Americans have this lesson to learn; Where justice is denied, where poverty is enforced, where ignorance prevails, and where any one class is made to feel that society is in an organized conspiracy to oppress, rob, and degrade them, neither persons nor property will be safe."—**Frederick Douglass** (1845) *A narrative of the life of Frederick Douglass, an American slave.*

"Sixty years ago I knew everything; now I know nothing; education is a progressive discovery of our own ignorance."—**Will Durant**, https://www.forbes.com/quotes/9701/

"The challenge of social justice is to evoke a sense of community that we need to make our nation a better place, just as we make it a safer place."—**Marian Wright Edelman**, https://www.uua.org/files/documents/aw/sje_handbook.pdf

"In place of equal respect, the nation offered women the Miss America beauty pageant, established in 1920–the same year women won the vote." —**Susan Faludi** (1991) Backlash: The undeclared war against American women.

"Any attempt to disturb the deadly routine of instruction is looked upon as sabotage. And the notion that the aims and functions of education should be determined in the local community by a close and continuous discussion among students, faculty, administration, and citizens is so visionary that it is not even seriously considered." —**Charles Ferguson** (n.d.). AZQuotes.com. https://www.azquotes.com/quote/546615

"The test of a first-rate intelligence is the ability to hold two opposed ideas in the mind at the same time, and still retain the ability to function. One should, for example, be able to see that things are hopeless and yet be determined to make them otherwise." —**F. Scott Fitzgerald** (February 1936) "The Crack-up," Esquire.

"All children have preparedness, potential, curiosity and interest in constructing their learning, in engaging in social interaction and in negotiating with everything the environment brings to them." —**Lella Gandini** (1993) Fundamentals of the Reggio Emilia approach to early childhood education, Young Children 49(1) 4–8. p 49.

"It is not who you attend school with but who controls the school you attend." —**Nikki Giovani**, https://twitter.com/nikki_gio/status/328621996957110272

"A teacher who can arouse a feeling for one single good action, for one single good poem, accomplishes more than he who fills our memory with rows and rows of natural objects, classified with name and form." —**Johann Wolfgang von Goethe** (1809) Elective Affinities.

"By the time they reach second grade, every child in the country knows what an Indian is. They wear lots of feathers, ride spotted ponies and shoot arrows. Indians who don't fit the type are invisible; they simply can't be imagined by the majority of White children or adults." —**Rayna Green**, https://scholarworks.iu.edu/dspace/bitstream/handle/2022/2398/ 31%282%29%2033-46.pdf?sequence=1&isAllowed=y

"I am only one, but still I am one. I cannot do everything, but still I can do something and because I cannot do everything, I will not refuse to do the something that I can do." —**Edward Everett Hale**, https://www.forbes.com/quotes/2504/

"So far, we do not seem appalled at the prospect of exactly the same kind of education being applied to all the school children from the Atlantic to the Pacific, but there is an uneasiness in the air, a realization that the individual is growing less easy to find; an idea, perhaps, of what standardization might become when the units are not machines, but human beings." —**Edith Hamilton** in Thruelsen, R. & Kobler, J. (Eds.) (1959) Adventures of the Mind, *Saturday Evening Post.*

"...one of the many uses of theory in academic locations is in the production of an intellectual class hierarchy where the only work deemed truly theoretical is work that is highly abstract, jargonistic, difficult to read, and containing obscure references...any theory that cannot be shared in everyday conversation cannot be used to educate the public," —**bell hooks** (1994) *Teaching to transgress: Education as the practice of freedom.*

"There are times when personal experience keeps us from reaching the mountain top and so we let it go because the weight of it is too heavy. And sometimes the mountain top is difficult to reach with all our resources, factual and confessional, so we are just there, collectively grasping, feeling the limitations of knowledge, longing together, yearning for a way to reach that highest point. Even this yearning is a way to know." —**bell hooks** (1994) *Teaching to transgress: Education as the practice of freedom.*

"If any female feels she need anything beyond herself to legitimate and validate her existence, she is already giving away her power to be self-defining, her agency." —**bell hooks**, https://www.usatoday.com/story/entertainment/celebrities/2021/1 2/15/bell-hooks-quotes-books-love-feminism/8910938002/

"No black woman writer in this culture can write 'too much.' Indeed, no woman writer can write 'too much' ... No woman has ever written enough." —**bell hooks** (1999) *Remembered rapture: The writer at work*.

"Sometimes, I feel discriminated against, but it does not make me angry. It merely astonishes me. How can any deny themselves the pleasure of my company? It's beyond me."—**Zora Neale Hurston**, https://harford.libguides.com/c.php?g=321439

"Most ignorance is vincible ignorance. We don't know because we don't want to know." —**Aldous Huxley** in Baker, R. & Sexton, J. (Eds.) (2001) *Aldous Huxley: Complete essays, Vol 4: 1936– 1938*, Ivan R Dee.

"Tell me the weight of a snowflake," a coalmouse asked a wild dove. "Nothing more than nothing," the dove answered. "In that case I must tell you a marvelous story," the coalmouse said. "I sat on a fir branch close to the trunk when it began to snow. Not heavily, not in a raging blizzard. No, just like in a dream, without any violence at all. Since I didn't have anything better to do, I counted the snowflakes settling on the twigs and needles of my branch. Their number was exactly 3,471,952. When the next snowflake dropped onto the branch—nothing more than nothing—as you say—the branch broke off." Having said that, the coalmouse ran away. The dove, since Noah's time an authority on peace, thought about the story for a while. Finally, she said to herself, "Perhaps there is only one person's voice lacking for peace to come to the world." —Kurt Kauter, New fables: Thus spoke the caribou.

"Though people with disabilities have become more vocal in recent years, we still constitute a very small minority. Yet the Beautiful People—the slender, fair and perfect ones—form a minority that may be even smaller." —**Deborah Kent** (1987) *Disabled U.S.A.* President's Committee on Employment of the Handicapped.

"We shall overcome because the arc of the moral universe is long but it bends toward justice." —**Dr. Martin Luther King, Jr**.

"I have almost reached the regrettable conclusion that the Negro's great stumbling block in his[*sic*]stride toward freedom is not the White Citizen's "Councilor" or the Ku Klux Klanner, but the white moderate who is more devoted to "order" than to justice; who prefers a negative peace which is the absence of tension to a positive peace which is the presence of justice; who constantly says "I agree with you in the goal you seek, but I cannot agree with your methods of direct action" who paternalistically believes he[*sic*] can set the timetable for another man's[*sic*] freedom; who lives by a mythical concept of time and who constantly advises the Negro to wait for a "more convenient season." —**Dr. Martin Luther King, Jr**. (1963) "Letter from a Birmingham Jail."

"An individual has not started living until he[*sic*] can rise above the narrow confines of his[*sic*] individualistic concerns to the broader concerns of all humanity." —**Dr. Martin Luther King, Jr.**, https://www.edi.nih.gov/people/sep/blacks/campaigns/mlk-observance-2022

"More money is put into prisons than into schools. That, in itself, is the description of a nation bent on suicide. I mean, what is more precious to us than our own children? We are going to build a lot more prisons if we do not deal with the schools and their inequalities." —**Jonathan Kozol** (1992) *Savage Inequalities: Children in America's Schools*, Harper Perennial.

"In the end, as any successful teacher will tell you, you can only teach the things that you are. If we practice racism then it is racism we teach." —**Max Lerner** (1949) "We Teach What We Are," *Actions and passions*.

"Your silence will not protect you." —**Audre Lorde** (1984) The Transformation of Silence into Language and Action, *Sister outsider: Essays and speeches*. The Crossing Press.

"One of the first things I think young people, especially nowadays, should learn is how to see for yourself and listen for yourself and think for yourself. Then you can come to an intelligent decision for yourself. If you form the habit of going by what you hear others say about someone, or going by what others think about someone, instead of searching that thing out for yourself and seeing for yourself, you will be walking west when you think you're going east, and you will be walking east when you think you're going west." — **Malcolm X** (1965) https://www.themilitant.com/2011/7520/752049.html

"Emancipate yourself from mental slavery. None but ourselves can free our mind." —**Bob Marley**, "Redemption Song," lyrics are from a 1937 speech delivered by Black rights activist **Marcus Garvey** in Sydney, Nova Scotia.

"When [a person] tells you he[sic] got rich through hard work, ask him[sic]: Whose?" —**Don Marquis**, https://quoteinvestigator.com/2020/01/01/hard-work/

"Always remember that you are absolutely unique. Just like everyone else." —**Margaret Mead** (1979) in Peers, J. & Bennett, G. (Eds.) *1,001 logical laws, accurate axioms, profound principles, trusty truisms, homey homilies, colorful corollaries, quotable quotes, and rambunctious ruminations for all walks of life.*

"Never doubt that a small group of thoughtful, committed citizens can change the world: Indeed, it's the only thing that ever has." — **Margaret Mead**, https://americanhistory.si.edu/collections/search/object/nmah_1285394

"The function of freedom is to free someone else." —**Toni Morrison** (1979) Barnard College commencement speech.

"In this country American means White. Everybody else has to hyphenate." —**Toni Morrison** (29 January 1992) *The Guardian*.

"Diversity is being invited to the party: Inclusion is being asked to dance." —**Vernā Myers**, https://www.vernamyers.com/2017/02/04/diversity-doesnt-stick-without-inclusion/

"Illegal aliens have always been a problem in the United States. Ask any Indian." —**Robert Orben** (14 March 1985) *Kokomo Tribune* (IN), "Celebrity Cipher," p. 32, col. 2.

"There must be those among whom we can sit down and weep, and still be counted as warriors." —**Adrienne Rich** (1983) *Sources.*

"We must all do our part, show up, speak up, do not tolerate hate or injustice. Be bold, be brave and be inspirational." —**Nina Roberts**, Dr. Nina Roberts homepage: San Francisco State University.

"Was putting a man on the moon actually easier than improving education in our public schools?" —**BF Skinner** (2002) *Beyond freedom and dignity*, Hackett.

"It is the greatest of all mistakes, to do nothing because you can only do a little." —**Sydney Smith** (1850) Lecture XIX: On the Conduct of the Understanding, Part II, *Elementary sketches of moral philosophy.*

The first problem for all of us, men and women, is not to learn, but to unlearn." —**Gloria Steinem**, https://www.nytimes.com/1971/08/26/archives/a-new-egalitarian-life-style.html?searchResultPosition=1

"If you are neutral in situations of injustice, you have chosen the side of the oppressor." —**Desmond Tutu** in Brown, R. M. (1984) *Unexpected news: Reading the Bible with third world eyes*, p. 19.

"I myself have never been able to find out what feminism is; I only know that people call me a feminist whenever I express sentiments that differentiate me from a doormat or a prostitute." —**Rebecca West**, (14 November 1913) "Mr. Chesterton in Hysterics," *The Clarion*, republished in *The Young Rebecca: Writings of Rebecca West*, 1911–17 (1982), p. 219.

"There may be times when we are powerless to prevent injustice, but there must never be a time when we fail to protest." —**Dr. Elie Wiesel** (December 11, 1986) Hope, despair and memory, Nobel Lecture. https://www.nobelprize.org/prizes/peace/1986/wiesel/lecture/

Contributor Biographies

Photo courtesy of Pathfinder Outdoor Education

Contributor Biographies

Esther Ayers, is a PhD candidate at Michigan State University in Chicano Latino Studies Program. Esther's education endeavors encompass receiving a masters in interpersonal practice and a minor in social policy and evaluation at the University of Michigan School of Social Work. Her current research interests are in mental health, Latina/x, and adventure therapy infusing a decolonial epistemology to amplify voices of historically underrepresented groups at nonprofit agencies. In addition to research interests Esther applies 9 years of clinical work experiences that weaved in adventure therapy techniques to guide her research. Then, in 2020 Esther was accepted to present with SEER, also she was an ActivatEE keynote speaker where Esther shared her testimonio of how mental health influenced her childhood and shed light on how she maneuvered those mental health experiences to guide her research. Esther carves out time to embrace family, spend time outdoors, and engage with outreach services.

Susie Barr-Wilson grew up camping and panning for gold with her grandpa in Washington state. She has been leading outdoor and experiential education programs for over 25 years. A graduate of Western Washington University's Recreation Department, Susie worked as program director at Lazy F Camp in central Washington and served as a Peace Corp volunteer in rural South Africa. She holds a master's degree in recreation from San Francisco State University and enjoys teaching alongside her former professors. Since 2010 Susie has worked with GirlVentures, an outdoor adventure organization for girls and nonbinary youth, including the positions of program manager, instructor, and course director. Susie has advised courses for Outward Bound California, and she is a graduate of the NOLS Rocky Mountain Outdoor Educator Course. Susie is published in the *Journal of Outdoor Recreation, Education, and Leadership*, and *The Palgrave International Handbook of Women and Outdoor Learning*.

M. Deborah Bialeschki, PhD, is Professor Emerita from the University of North Carolina-Chapel Hill and Senior Researcher Emerita from the American Camp Association (ACA). During her career, she has authored 15 books, collaborated on 20 book chapters, and contributed numerous articles and presentations to national and international journals and conferences. Deb has been editor of major research journals, has chaired national research conferences, and has been elected to professional academies. She received academic awards including the Tanner Faculty Award for Excellence in Undergraduate Teaching from UNC-Chapel Hill, the Society for Park and Recreation Educators (SPRE) National Award for Excellence in Teaching, and the SPRE Distinguished Colleague Award. Deb's research has focused on youth development through outdoor and camp experiences, staff training and development, program quality, and women's issues in leisure and outdoor recreation. Over her career, Deb has been committed to diversity, equity, inclusion, and social justice of youth and adults in all aspects of life.

Lise Brown is a mother, sister, daughter and auntie living in Treaty One Territory, win-nipi, manitowapow, Kanata, also known as Winnipeg, Manitoba, Canada. Lise is a co-owner of a 100% female owned and operated organization called Momenta Inc., also a certified B corp. At Momenta, Lise provides counseling, clinical direction, consulting, and support for individuals, families, community organizations, and Momenta's staff. Momenta was founded in 2007 with the goal of creating experiences that discover strengths and foster growth. Lise has a Master of Social Work and a Bachelor of Recreation Management and is a Forest School Practitioner and Trainer. She is guided by her organization's values of have fun, take care of each other, be respectful, join in and be safe and is strengths based, trauma informed and antioppressive in her work as an adventure therapist.

Dr. **Mary Breunig** has spent the last two decades as an outdoor recreation professor and Director of Social Justice and Equity Studies programs at Canadian universities. She recently started teaching at California State University-Sacramento on the traditional and ancestral homelands of the Miwok, Wintu, Maidu, Nisenan (southern Maidu), and Patwin Native peoples. Her scholarship focuses on social and environmental justice, schoolyard pedagogy, student-directed teaching and learning, and Freirian praxis. Mary is a NOLS and Outward Bound instructor. She is a climber, cyclist, avid paddler, place-based enthusiast, and urban flaneur. Find out more at marybreunig.com

Bethany Facendini's mission is to strive for social justice and environmental sustainability for all. Bethany is passionate about working alongside communities furthest from opportunities to build resiliency and overcome disparities through innovative upstream approaches. She has over 25 years of professional experience specializing in community engagement, experiential education, youth development, and grassroots organizing in the San Francisco Bay Area and beyond. Bethany has led justice, equity, and inclusion efforts in the field of experiential education at California State Parks, East Bay Regional Parks, and Sonoma County Regional Parks. She has a bachelor's degree from the University of California at Berkeley, a master's degree in environmental and social justice from Sonoma State University, and an urban environmental education certificate from Cornell University. Bethany is a member of Government Alliance on Race and Equity and Showing Up for Racial Justice, and has served on the County of Sonoma's Racial Equity Core Team and Latino Service Providers board. She is currently traveling the world creating global community.

Carolyn Finney, PhD, is a storyteller and cultural geographer who works at the intersection of the arts (pursued an acting career for eleven years), education (Fulbright and National Science Scholar Fellow), and lived experience and is an artist-in-residence at Middlebury College. A national and international speaker on difference, identity, belonging, and place, she has written for numerous outlets including the *NY Times*, *The Guardian* and *Outside Magazine*, and is the author of *Black Faces, White Spaces: Reimagining the Relationship of African Americans to the Great Outdoors* (2014). Recently awarded the Alexander and Ilse Melamid Medal from the American Geographical Society, she is currently working on a new book (a more personal journey into the relationship between race, land, and belonging) and a performance piece entitled The N Word: Nature, Revisited as part of an Andrew W. Mellon residency at the New York Botanical Gardens Humanities Institute.

Dan Garvey is the Executive Dean for the Spring 2023 voyage of Semester at Sea. Previously, he was President/Professor Emeritus of

Prescott College. Dan was a faculty member and administrator at the University of New Hampshire for 16 years. He was also the Executive Director of the Association for Experiential Education. He's the recipient of the The Kurt Hahn Address Award and Julian Smith Award. He was a member of the first planning committee that helped create AmeriCorps. Dan has worked with projects in Russia, South Africa, Taiwan, Tanzania, and Israel. He received his PhD from the University of Colorado, Master of Arts from Cambridge/Goddard Graduate School for Social Change. He is currently Trustee for Semester at Sea. Previously, he served as Trustee of NOLS and Project Adventure.

Michael Gass, PhD, LMFT, CCAT, CCBT, is a Professor in the College of Health and Human Services at the University of New Hampshire. He received his Ph.D. from the University of Colorado at Boulder and completed postdoctoral studies in marriage and family therapy. Dr. Gass currently directs two critical research initiatives in the field of adventure therapy—one as Director of the Outdoor Behavioral Healthcare Research Center (OBHRC) and another as Director of the NATSAP Research Database. He has made over 400 professional presentations and written over 250 professional publications. His book, *Effective Programming in Adventure Programming* written with Dr. Simon Priest, is the largest selling textbook in the field. His latest book, written with Dr. Lee Gillis and Dr. Keith Russell, *Adventure Therapy: Theory, Research, and Practice*, was published by Routledge Press in 2020.

Sarita Gray is a college student and works for Sonoma County Regional Parks as an open water lifeguard in Northern California. Among other things she has worked hard in the parks to advocate for justice, equity, diversity, and inclusion for all. She has grown up in the experiential education world and that has given her the opportunity to meet some phenomenal mentors. She is currently preparing to set sail with Semester at Sea in January of 2023 and looks forward to many multicultural learning opportunities and grand adventures across the globe.

Sky Gray is the Program Manager for the Valley of the Moon Children's Center for the Sonoma County Human Services Department. She is a fierce advocate for children and youth, as well an advocate for diversity, equity, and inclusion (DEI). She is a master trainer on Adverse Childhood Experience and a trainer in Trauma Informed Care. She advances transformative work through the use of trauma informed principles and practices and serves on the Racial Equity committee for Sonoma County. Throughout her career she worked closely with the late Dr. Nina Roberts (Roberts, Gray and Associates) doing DEI consulting and humanistic risk management. Sky was the former longest standing executive director of the nationally known and accredited Mountain Center where she broke the glass ceiling. She has been a member of Association for Experiential Education (AEE) since 1984, served as the AEE Director of Accreditation, served on the WRMC, as well as on the AEE BOD.

William Woodrow "Bill" Gwaltney is a seventh generation native of Washington, D.C. Descended from African American soldiers, sailors, farmers, and teachers, Gwaltney attended College in Ohio and University in Maryland. Gwaltney worked for nearly four decades in positions in the National Park Service across the nation, the National Museum of African American History and Culture in the Nation's Capital, and for the American Battle Monuments Commission serving overseas American Military Cemeteries with offices in Paris, France. While with the National Park Service, he developed a number of diversity outreach and recruiting programs and created several museum exhibits focusing on African American history. Now officially retired, Gwaltney has served on a number of national boards of directors and was a faculty/mentor with the University of Missouri at St. Louis, where he was engaged teaching online in the Heritage Leadership Program, which was focused on education, social justice, community leadership, and heritage commemoration.

McClellan (Mac) Hall is of Cherokee ancestry. He is the founder and executive director of the National Indian Youth Leadership Project. Mac holds a Master's in Education from Arizona State University. He served on the SAMHSA Native American Center for Excellence Expert Panel on Prevention and was colead of the American Indian/ Alaska Native Task Force on Suicide Prevention. Mac is the developer of Project Venture, recognized as the Most Effective program for Native American youth in SAMHSA's National High Risk Youth Study. He and his wife of 44 years, live in Santa Fe, NM, where they help their raise grandchildren. Mac is the recipient of several awards, including the Kurt Hahn Honoree from AEE; the Spirit of Crazy Horse Award; the Alice King Public Service Award; the Alec Dickson Servant Leader Award; and the Indian Health Service Director's Behavioral Health Achievement award. Currently, Mac is doing consultant work with several organizations.

Chris Heeter is a wilderness guide, keynote speaker, dog musher, and poet. She started The Wild Institute (www.thewildinstitute.com) in 2001, guiding canoeing and dogsledding trips and taking what she learns in the outdoors to offices and conferences as a professional speaker, focusing on leadership, teamwork, inclusion, and work culture. Featured on The Discovery Channel's 'National Geographic Today,' she's been guiding trips since 1983 and still, somehow, loves to portage. She sits on the board of MCEA (Minnesota Center for Environmental Advocacy). She holds a bachelor's degree from George Williams College in recreation, with an emphasis in social work, and was a recipient of the distinguished alumni award.

Karla A. Henderson, PhD, is currently Professor Emerita in the Department of Parks, Recreation, and Tourism Management at North Carolina State University. She was on the faculty at the University of North Carolina at Chapel Hill, University of Wisconsin-Madison, and Texas Woman's University. Her Ph.D. was completed at the University of Minnesota. In 2012 she received an honorary doctorate from the University of Waterloo in Ontario, Canada. Karla served as coeditor of *Leisure Sciences* and on the editorial boards of numerous leisure and outdoor related journals. She contributed to the profession by serving as president of organizations such as SPRE, AAHPERD Research Consortium, and The Academy of Leisure Sciences. Now retired, Karla enjoys hiking and snowshoeing in the Rocky Mountains, volunteering at her beloved Rocky Mountain National Park, playing her trumpet, being entertained by her two ferocious cats, and reading and writing whenever she has a chance.

Margaret Lechner's career was influenced by her naturalist mother and mountaineer father. For 30+ years Margaret was associated with Earlham College, first as a student, then as Jill-of-all-trades on the faculty. Her roles included student staff on August Wilderness, cofounder of Southwest Field Studies and of the East Africa semester, director of the Wilderness Program, teaching biology and education, and facilitating Quaker Foundations of Leadership. She served on the AEE board of directors from 1990 to 1996. Margaret left Earlham to develop a community mediation center, then became a full-time volunteer with AVP (Alternatives to Violence Project). Her Covid-time project was organizing the 50th anniversary celebration of the Earlham Wilderness Program, including coauthoring *They Kindled a Fire: The First 50 Years of Wilderness at Earlham College.* Margaret delights in her children (one biological and many whom she has mentored), family and friends, bread baking, fabric arts, and Tai Chi at sunrise.

Former Captain **Aniko Kannas-Millan** enjoyed 28 years with Santa Clara County Parks before retiring as a Park Ranger Supervisor. Her efforts were to diversify both the workplace and park visitation through promotion and education and, thereby, also increase the number of people of color who enjoy our public spaces. Aniko is currently with Friends of Santa Cruz County Parks as a Parks Specialist doing precisely this work! She assists community leaders to bring their engagement efforts to life, primarily through outdoor recreation programming activities. It's so important that all people feel welcomed to go outside and experience the benefits of nature and outdoor spaces. If we want to improve our mental and physical health and overall well being then parks offer a free opportunity to do so. Aniko's focus is to continue this consistent messaging to our communities and agencies to make it happen!

Dr. **Pavlína Látková** is a Professor in the Department of Recreation, Parks, and Tourism at San Francisco State University. She has been researching tourism planning and development for over 19 years, specializing in sustainable community-based tourism in rural and urban communities. Dr. Látková is an advocate for socially responsible travel experiences that promote cultural understanding, fulfill personal dreams, and encourage environmental sustainability. She teaches multiple tourism and professional development courses which incorporate experiential and service-learning that contribute to high academic achievement and prepare students for careers in recreation, parks, and tourism. Collaborating with the San Francisco Bay Area community partners, Dr. Látková creates field-based experiences that expose students to practitioners with different backgrounds and experiences, including local small business owners and entrepreneurs. In addition, she has developed and led faculty-led study abroad programs to domestic and international destinations, which students describe as "life-changing experiences."

Dr. **TA Loeffler** brings over 35 years of expertise leading people through significant life-changing experiences to every facet of their work. TA's adventures have taken them to 52 different countries and all seven continents. TA has completed 6 and 4/5 of "The Seven Summits," the highest peak on all seven continents. In 2020, TA was named to the "Canada's 90 Greatest Explorers List" by Canadian Geographic. As a Professor of Outdoor Education at Memorial University, TA has developed a reputation for excellence in experiential education because their students are more likely to be outside chasing icebergs than sitting in a classroom. TA has received recognition for innovative experiential teaching. TA was named a 3M National Teaching Fellow in 2008. From AEE, TA received the Karl Rohnke Creativity Award (2007), the Outstanding Experiential Teacher of the Year (1999), and was selected to deliver the Marina Ewald and Kurt Hahn Address in 2018.

D. Maurie Lung, PhD, LMHC, LMFT, integrates almost 30 years of experience in recreation, education, psychology, and evaluation to provide therapeutic services in a community-based organization she founded, Life Adventures, and is the Director of Adventure-based and Nature-based Counseling programs at Prescott College. Additionally, Maurie consults with organizations, supervises mental health interns, presents internationally, and is an author of both books and articles in this field. Maurie utilizes experiential methodology to provide services with a diverse client population. The growth and change she witnesses for youth, families, and adults through this process continues to amaze her and remind her of the power of playful experience.

Dr. **Kynetta Sugar McFarlane**, PsyD, (she/her/hers) is a clinical psychologist and the creator/owner of Transformative Health, LLC, where she provides trauma-informed and affirming therapeutic services. Dr. McFarlane is half African-American and Guyanese and started working on her advanced degrees as the single parent of a 2-year-old. She has been identified as an expert in trauma in federal court. Dr. McFarlane completed a predoctoral internship with a focus

231

on trauma and adventure group therapy and a postdoctoral fellowship in complex trauma. She is also an expert in the treatment of SOGIE. Dr. McFarlane is the System of Care, Equity and Inclusion Coordinator for The Center for Innovative Practices (CIP) at Case Western Reserve University's Mandel School of Applied Social Sciences. She is an expert on the Project ECHO Team at Northeast Ohio Medical University. She has spoken to national and international audiences on issues related to trauma, culture, and gender diversity.

Priscilla McKenney has a rich professional history of guiding in the Himalayas, teaching climbing and mountaineering in the North Cascades and California, and leading sea kayak expeditions in Alaska and Baja. Starting with Outward Bound and Woodswomen in the 80's, she has worked with a broad spectrum of groups from college students and adults to youth, as director, trainer, and instructor. Much of her work has focused on supporting and directing outdoor programs for women and girls. Her eight years as Program Director for GirlVentures established her reputation as an influential leader in girls' outdoor programs and leadership development. She has published in various academic publications, been a regular AEE conference presenter and served as adjunct faculty at San Francisco State University and Prescott College. She has also been an advocate, ally, and leader in addressing issues of diversity, equity, and inclusion in the field of adventure education.

Binky Martin-Tollette is an Assistant Director at Joseph Pfeifer Kiwanis Camp based in Little Rock, Arkansas. She prefers making programs work, building relationships, and putting her whole self into logistics. Binky has presented workshops at AEE conferences, hosted regional conferences and was the convenor for the AEE International Conference at Little Rock, AR. She is a member of the American Camp Association and the Association of Experiential Education. She is married and has two sons and two daughters.

Lara Mendel is the Executive Director and Cofounder of The Mosaic Project which teaches people, from elementary school students to adults in the workplace, the skills they need to build the diverse, inclusive communities they envision. Since 2000, Mosaic has provided over 75,000 individuals with immersive, experiential education programs in equity, empathy, and effective communication across differences. Prior to founding Mosaic, Lara had a brief career in cross-species communication working with gorillas, monkeys, and dolphins. She then worked extensively in youth development and cross-cultural communication on four continents. She also taught violence prevention and self-defense and is a Black Belt in Kajukenbo Kung Fu. Lara received a BA and MA in anthropology from Stanford University.

Denise Mitten, PhD is a widely experienced international adventure guide, from SCUBA to mountaineering (Swiss Alps, Himalayas, and USA, including Denali) and more. Denise initiated trauma informed leadership highlighting the relevance of emotional and spiritual safety in group dynamics and risk management, first working with women recovering from abuse in the early 1980s. She developed programs to strengthen bonding between parents/caregivers and children, a leadership program for women felons, and an award-winning leadership training and apprenticing program for women, opening the door to outdoor leadership to many women. Denise received the Dr. Martin Luther King, Jr. Social Justice Award from Ferris State University for her efforts around wellness for underserved groups. Denise has been the AEE BOD president and treasurer and served on their Accreditation Council and as an associate editor for the *Journal of Experiential Education*. In 2011, Denise offered the Marina Ewald and Kurt Hahn Address. She loves being a mom and being outdoors.

Lauren Mitten grew up half in the outdoors, half in the books, and entirely in the upper Midwest. They expanded their horizons at college in Southern California, and moved to Washington, DC, where they stay because they love the architecture and the street grid system. Lauren currently runs a mobile bicycle repair operation, with goals that include empowering customers to do as much of their own bike work as they want, reducing fossil fuel reliance, demystifying bicycle mechanics, and being a visibly queer mechanic.

Christine Lynn Norton, PhD, LCSW-S, she/her/hers, is a Professor of Social Work at Texas State University. She received her PhD in Social Work from Loyola University Chicago. She has a MA in Social Service Administration from the University of Chicago, and a MS in Experiential Education from Minnesota State University-Mankato.

She is a Certified Clinical Trauma Professional, a Certified Experiential Therapist, a Certified Clinical Adventure Therapist. Christine has over 30 years of experience as a social worker and outdoor experiential educator. Christine is a research scientist with the Outdoor Behavioral Healthcare Center and was a 2017 Fulbright Scholar, having taught adventure therapy at National Taiwan Normal University. Christine leads resilience trainings focused on mental health, trauma recovery, and the healing power of nature, and she has presented her work around the world. She is also an ActivatEE storytelling coach for the Association for Experiential Education.

Tanya Rao, MS, is passionate about bringing life-changing experiences to people from all backgrounds through outdoor adventures. During her graduate program, Tanya's research centered on bringing outdoor adventure education to adolescent girls and women, especially from diverse cultural backgrounds. She has presented her research at conferences held by the California Parks and Recreation Society (2011, 2014) and the Association for Experiential Education (2012, 2015). Tanya has led several backpacking trips with girls and women of all ages through San Francisco State University, GirlVentures, and Call of the Wild Adventures, and mentored young women in developing outdoor leadership skills. She has worked as the Latin America sales specialist for Mountain Travel Sobek, a pioneer in adventure travel around the world. In addition to being a mother, currently, Tanya is running her family's Indian coffee business in the San Francisco area.

Alyssa Roberts is a communications lawyer and mom of two beautiful young adults. She spends her weekends volunteering at an animal shelter and enjoys hiking, reading, and making crooked pots at a local ceramic studio. With frequent moves growing up, Alyssa was happy to be known as "Nina's little sister." Alyssa eventually landed on the east coast, and Nina on the west, but they didn't let the miles keep them apart. They shared a love of nature and a strong sense of family. She misses her sister tremendously but takes comfort in many fond memories, in knowing that Nina lived an incredible life, and that there is no end to the good she has done. Alyssa lives in Northern Virginia with her two pups and various critters in cages her daughter acquired but did not take to college.

Stuart Slay serves as the Senior Director of Risk and Safety at the Student Conservation Association (SCA), where he also represents the SCA on the Wilderness Risk Management Conference steering committee. Prior to serving with the SCA, Stuart directed Chadwick International School's Outdoor Education Program in South Korea, where he worked for nearly 10 years. In Korea, Stuart worked to build an outdoor education program in a unique, Korean context. From this work he pursued a master's degree in adventure education from Prescott College, with a focus on identifying and assessing risks stemming from cultural factors. Stuart's background includes ski patrolling, guiding, and avalanche forecasting in Northern California and the Andes mountains of Chile, and field instructing with the Northwest and California Outward Bound Schools and several school-based programs. Stuart currently resides in Tacoma, WA.

During his nearly 40 years of experience with the National Park Service (NPS), **Bob Stanton** served as a seasonal park ranger, management assistant, park superintendent, deputy regional director, regional director, associate director, and director, giving him a perspective and depth of experience matched by few others. He was born in Fort Worth, Texas, and grew up in a small African American community in the Mosier Valley. His modest upbringing and his experiences early in life helped shape both his character and his career choices. He earned a Bachelor of Science degree from Huston-Tillotson University in 1963, the first in his immediate family to graduate from college. He later did graduate work at Boston University and George Washington University. Stanton's career with the NPS began in 1962 when the secretary of the interior appointed him as a summer seasonal park ranger at Grand Teton National Park in Wyoming.

Amelia Tarren is an avid adventurer and climber living in Burlington, Vermont. She has a B.A. from Hampshire College in environmental science and an M.S. from the University of Vermont in mathematics. She works as an applied mathematician with the Department of Veterans Affairs and Harvard Medical School. A favorite math problem is tackling the occasional geometrically curious climbing crux at the local crag. She enjoyed growing up in the Connecticut River Valley of western Massachusetts and maintains a strong connection with northeastern outdoor communities including the Western Mass

Climbers Coalition, Outdoor Asian, and the Association for Experiential Education. Her favorite trips include kayaking with whales in Alaska, snorkeling in Australia's Great Barrier Reef, mountaineering in the Peruvian Andes, and climbing throughout the world.

Charles Thomas, being of African American, Japanese, and Native American descent, has dedicated his life to promoting diversity inclusion in the outdoors and is the Executive Director of Outward Bound Adventures Inc (OBA). For 40 years, he has created education programs that have provided thousands of historically absent BIPOC youths and families access to outdoor recreation, conservation, and environmental education. OBA's diverse participants have gone on to staff a multitude of agencies and organizations, such as the US Forest Service, NPS, Bureau of Land Management, and retailers like REI and Patagonia. In recognition of his lifelong effort in creating outdoor equitable inclusion and diversification, he has been honored by U.S. Congressional Representatives, State Senates, and community-based organizations and invited to the White House to witness President Obama signing the America's Great Outdoor Initiative. His book, *Urban Spaces to Wild Places* is scheduled for release in 2023.

Sanford Tollette is the Executive Director of Joseph Pfeifer Kiwanis Camp in Little Rock, Arkansas. He received a B.S. in early childhood education from the University of Arkansas. He has presented workshops at AEE conferences and served on the AEE Board of directors. He received the AEE Michael Stratton Outstanding Practitioner's Award and was selected as a Marina Ewald and Kurt Hahn Address presenter. Sanford was recognized by President Obama as a White House Champion of Change. He has also received the Human and Civil Rights Citizen Award from the Arkansas Education Association. He is a member of the American Camp Association, and the Association of Experiential Education. Currently, he serves on the Child Welfare Agency Licensing Review Board of the Arkansas Department of Human Services and on the Central High Museum Board. He is married and has two sons and two daughters.

Anita R. Tucker, PhD, LICSW is a Professor of Social Work at the University of New Hampshire. Since her mid 20s she has been involved in the world of experiential education and in particular, adventure therapy (AT). She teaches graduate research classes and AT facilitation and these skills are highlighted in her 40+ peer reviewed publications on adventure therapy and her recent textbook on AT facilitation, *Adventure Group Psychotherapy*. As a licensed clinical social worker, she has experience running AT programs with youth involved in the foster care, mental health, and juvenile justice systems. As a scholar, Dr. Tucker believes in the importance of research-practitioner partnerships so that research is applicable and meaningful to the clients served. She has been a volunteer leader for AEE and AEE's Therapeutic Adventure Professional Group since 2003 and finds immense joy in collaborating with AT practitioners and students.

Karen Warren, PhD, has spent almost 50 years in outdoor experiential education, including teaching courses in experiential education, outdoor leadership, wilderness studies, and social justice for 36 years at Hampshire College in Amherst, MA. She has led students on hundreds of trips all over the world. Karen has written, presented, and spoken extensively on social justice and gender issues in outdoor experiential education. Her books include *Theory and Practice of Experiential Education*, *Women's Voices in Experiential Education*, and *The Theory of Experiential Education*. Karen has been honored to receive the 1998 Michael Stratton Practitioner Award and the 2006 Outstanding Experiential Teacher Award from AEE. She has given the Josh Minor Address at the Northeast Regional AEE conference and the 2014 Marina Ewald and Kurt Hahn Address at the International AEE conference. Presently, Karen enjoys retirement with wide-ranging travel and works in her tiny house on writing projects including her outdoor travel blog, outdooradventuresampler.com.

Tameria M. Warren, PhD, is a native of Detroit, Michigan who has spent her career in various facets of the environmental field. Dr. Warren began her career as an environmental engineer with General Motors, then transitioned into a Department of Defense contractor performing environmental compliance and training with the military. Along the way, she became an adjunct professor with the University of South Carolina and eventually served as undergraduate studies coordinator for its School of the Earth, Ocean, and Environment (SEOE). She is currently an environmental specialist with Samsung Electronics and Home Appliances, the corporation's first manufacturing facility based in the United States. Her environmental work also extends into community engagement and education. Dr. Warren received a B.S. in environmental studies and applications from Michigan State University, a M.S. in environmental, health, and safety management from Rochester Institute of Technology, and a Ph.D. in sustainability education from Prescott College.

Sändra J. Washington is a City Councilperson in Lincoln, Nebraska and sits on the boards of Nebraska Trails Foundation, Lincoln Community Foundation, National Parks Conservation Association, and the Emeriti Board of American Association of State and Local History. Sändra worked with the National Park Service for nearly 25 years, holding positions in planning, training and development, environmental compliance, and as a park superintendent before becoming Midwest Chief of Planning. Highlights of her career include NPS Management Policies, 2001, and the creation of five new national park units. Sändra retired in 2014 as Associate Regional Director for the Midwest Region for Cultural Resources, Planning, Construction, Communications, Legislation & Congressional Affairs. She holds B.S and M.S. degrees from the Ohio State University, School of Natural Resources and is a lifetime member of Girl Scouts USA. Outdoor Highlights include Napali Coast of Kauai, Denali, and any night when I can see the Milky Way.

Sharon J. Washington, PhD, is a strategic leadership and organizational development consultant with nearly four decades of professional experience in higher education and nonprofit leadership, not-for-profit boards, K-12 education, experiential education, and the arts. Throughout her career Sharon has engaged in work that contributes to a greater understanding of individuals and groups and ways to foster greater equity and inclusion. Career highlights include Interim Provost at Mills College, Executive Director of the National Writing Project, Provost and Professor of Education at Spelman College, and tenured faculty appointments at Kent State University and Springfield College. Sharon's early work was facilitating New Games, leading outdoor trips for youth, and serving as the program director and instructor at an adventure education center. Her published writings are on leadership, multicultural alliances, equity in recreation and leisure studies, and the emotional and intellectual challenges of teaching about social justice. Outdoor highlights include Antarctica, Grand Canyon, and Patagonia.

Rita Yerkes is Principal of Yerkes Consulting LLC and works with board and fund development, collaborative planning, and DEIB presentations and training. Dr. Yerkes is Dean Emerita, George Williams College of Aurora University. She created innovative outdoor experiential education programs at Towson State University, Miami of Ohio University, State University of New York at Cortland, and Aurora University. She is a cofounder of the Coalition of Education in the Outdoors, past president of the Council on Outdoor Education, former chair of the Women's Professional Group in the AEE, past AEE board member, president, volunteer interim executive director, accreditation council chair and member. Rita is the 1998 Marina Ewald and Kurt Hahn presenter. She is a published author of numerous journal articles, presentations, and book chapters and coauthored, *Enduring Vision: From an Encampment to a Distinctive College a History of George Williams College 1884–1961.*

Aiko Yoshino, PhD, is a native of Japan, an experiential educator, a scholar, an immigrant, and a mother. She is an Associate Professor and teaches leadership, wellness, and outdoor recreation courses in the Department of Recreation, Parks, & Tourism at San Francisco State University (USA). Her scholarship is rooted in health and outdoor experiences through the lens of equity. Her work includes psychological resilience, nature-based chronic illness prevention in marginalized communities, health impacts of blue spaces, restorative experience through virtual reality experience. Dr. Yoshino is a former wilderness instructor for Wilderness Education Association, Outward Bound, and NOLS. She serves on the OBUSA Safety Board and the Multicultural Advisory Council for the largest regional park the East Bay Regional Park District. She enjoys going outside for hiking, paddling, climbing, biking, and, of course, picnicking with her loved ones.

239